W9-BBV-051

Donovan McNabb

FOOTBALL SUPERSTARS

Tiki Barber
Tom Brady
John Elway
Brett Favre
Peyton Manning
Dan Marino
Donovan McNabb
Joe Montana
Walter Payton
Jerry Rice
Ben Roethlisberger
Barry Sanders

FOOTBALL SUPERSTARS

Donovan McNabb

Richard Worth

CHELSEA HOUSE
PUBLISHERS
An imprint of Infobase Publishing

DONOVAN McNABB

Chelsea House
An imprint of Infobase Publishing
132 West 31st Street
New York NY 10001

Library of Congress Cataloging-in-Publication Data
Worth, Richard.
  Donovan Mcnabb / by Richard Worth.
    p. cm. — (Football superstars)
  Includes bibliographical references and index.
  ISBN 978-0-7910-9668-0 (hardcover)
  1. McNabb, Donovan—Juvenile literature. 2. Football players—United States—
Biography—Juvenile literature. 3. Quarterbacks (Football)—United States—Biography—
Juvenile literature. I. Title. II. Series.

  GV939.M38W67 2009
  796.332092—dc22
  [B]

314109

2008022236

Text design by Erik Lindstrom
Cover design by Ben Peterson

Printed in the United States of America

Bang EJB 10 9 8 7 6 5 4 3 2 1

This book is printed on acid-free paper.

CONTENTS

The Agony
of Defeat

On February 6, 2005, a crowd of more than 78,000 football fans jammed into Alltel Stadium in Jacksonville, Florida. It was a fairly mild evening with the temperature at almost 60°F (15.5°C) as they waited for the **kickoff** of Super Bowl XXXIX. The game featured a matchup between the New England Patriots, trying to become the first team to win three Super Bowls in four years, and the Philadelphia Eagles.

The Eagles had never won a Super Bowl. In the previous four years, the Eagles had rolled up outstanding regular-season records. They had gone to the playoffs, only to lose on their way to the Super Bowl. But this year might be different. Many Eagle fans, dressed in green and white jerseys—the team colors—had traveled to Jacksonville from Philadelphia. They were hoping that this year the Eagles would become the Super Bowl champions.

The Eagles were guided by coach Andy Reid and sixth-year **quarterback** Donovan McNabb, who was considered one of the best all-around quarterbacks in professional football. In 2004, he had thrown for more than 3,800 **yards** and completed 31 touchdown passes. But the 6-foot-2 inch, 240-pound (188-centimeter, 109-kilogram) McNabb was also a gifted rusher. He had gained 220 yards on the ground, scoring three **touchdowns**. McNabb had also been named **National Football Conference** (NFC) Offensive Player of the Year.

In their championship season, McNabb had led the Eagles to a 13–3 record and first place in the NFC East. McNabb and the Eagles then trounced the Minnesota Vikings 27-14 in the divisional playoffs. A week later, they handily won the NFC Championship Game, beating the Atlanta Falcons 27-10.

Besides McNabb, the Eagles had other powerful offensive weapons. McNabb's favorite target was **wide receiver** Terrell Owens. During the 2004 season, Owens had hauled in an impressive number of **receptions** before injuring his ankle in mid-December. He missed the rest of the regular season and the two playoff games but returned just in time for the Super Bowl. Besides Owens, the Eagles had wide receiver Todd Pinkston and **running backs** Brian Westbrook (who was also a threat as a receiver) and Dorsey Levens.

On defense, the Eagles boasted an impressive lineup with **cornerback** Lito Sheppard and **safeties** Michael Lewis and Brian Dawkins. Between the three of them, they had **sacked** opposing quarterbacks four times and hauled in ten **interceptions**. The defensive line was also very strong, pinning quarterbacks behind the **line of scrimmage** numerous times during the season.

The Eagles would need all of their offensive and defensive weapons if they expected to defeat the New England Patriots. Led by quarterback Tom Brady, the Patriots had already won two Super Bowls. They had eight consecutive postseason wins since 2001. Along with Brady, the Patriots had wide receivers Deion Branch and David Givens as well as running backs Corey Dillon and Kevin Faulk. The defense was also impressive, led by safety Rodney Harrison along with **linebackers** Tedy Bruschi and Willie McGinest. On their way to the Super Bowl, the Patriots had decisively beaten the Indianapolis Colts 20-3. Then they defeated the Pittsburgh Steelers in the **American Football Conference** (AFC) Championship Game 41-27.

A CLOSE GAME AND AN AGONIZING LOSS

In the first quarter, both teams battled back and forth trying to score the first touchdown. Late in the quarter, McNabb led his team down the field, sparked by a 30-yard completion to Owens. The Eagles drove to the Patriots' 8-yard line, when McNabb was sacked for a 16-yard loss. Another pass by McNabb was intercepted by Harrison at the 4-yard line. As the first quarter ended, neither team had scored.

After the start of the second quarter, according to Damon Hack of *The New York Times,* "McNabb started finding a rhythm with his throws." He engineered an 81-yard **drive**, including a 40-yard catch by Pinkston. Then "McNabb rocked in the **pocket** and fired waist high and [tight end L.J.] Smith corralled the pass for a touchdown." This gave the Eagles a 7-0 lead.

But the Patriots came right back later in the quarter. Eagles punter Dirk Johnson kicked a short 29-yard **punt**. This gave the Patriots the ball in Eagles territory, on the 37-yard line. A seven-play drive ended with Brady completing a four-yard touchdown pass to Givens. At the end of the first half, the game was tied 7-7.

As the second half opened, the Patriots began a 69-yard drive toward the Eagles' **goal line**. The march downfield was highlighted by four completions from Brady to Branch. Brady capped the drive with a two-yard pass to Mike Vrabel for the

Philadelphia Eagles quarterback Donovan McNabb leaped into the arms of center Hank Fraley after completing a seven-yard touchdown pass to tight end L.J. Smith in the second quarter of Super Bowl XXXIX. The touchdown gave the Eagles a 7-0 lead over the New England Patriots in the Super Bowl, held on February 6, 2005, in Jacksonville, Florida.

touchdown. The Patriots occasionally used Vrabel, who normally played linebacker, on offense in short-yardage situations. The Patriots had a 14-7 lead.

The Eagles tied the game late in the third period. McNabb engineered a 74-yard drive, featuring passes to Westbrook. According to reporter Damon Hack, "McNabb spotted running back Brian Westbrook streaking through the back of the **end zone**. McNabb rifled a pass between two defenders, and Westbrook pulled it in for a touchdown." The game was tied 14-14. As both teams entered the fourth quarter, no one could be sure of the outcome.

But late in the third quarter and early in the final quarter, the Patriots began to take control of the game. Brady led his team on a 66-yard drive. It featured running plays by Kevin Faulk and a two-yard touchdown rush by Corey Dillon. With only about 13 minutes left, the Patriots had a 21-14 lead. The Eagles' next possession was unsuccessful and led to a punt. The Patriots then put together a drive down the field, sparked by a 19-yard pass to Branch. The Patriots sent in their placekicker, Adam Vinatieri, who booted a 22-yard **field goal** to put New England ahead 24-14.

On the next drive, McNabb led the Eagles to the New England 36-yard line. His next pass, though, was intercepted by linebacker Tedy Bruschi on the 24-yard line. The Eagles were able to hold the Patriots, forcing them to punt. When Philadelphia finally began its next drive, time was running out, with less than six minutes to go. Still, the Eagles did not use a **no-huddle offense**—calling more than one play without a **huddle**—to save time.

Nevertheless, McNabb marched the Eagles down the field, covering 79 yards in 13 plays. McNabb found receiver Greg Lewis on a post pattern and completed a 31-yard touchdown pass. The Eagles had drawn within three points of the Patriots, but less than two minutes were left in the game.

Philadelphia tried an **onside kick**, hoping to get the ball back, but it was recovered by the Patriots. New England called a series of running plays to eat up the clock. Meanwhile, the Eagles used up their **timeouts** to stop the clock in the hope of getting back the football before the game ended. When the Patriots finally punted, less than a minute remained.

It wasn't enough time for Philadelphia to march from its own 4-yard line. McNabb tried a series of passes, hoping to make some quick strikes. But his third-down pass to **tight end** L.J. Smith was off-target and was intercepted by Harrison. As time ran out, the Eagles had come up short—24-21—and lost the Super Bowl.

AFTER THE GAME

With their third Super Bowl victory in four years, the Patriots were being called a dynasty. "Dynasty?" asked one Associated Press article on ESPN.com. "Definitely. The New England Patriots don't have to proclaim greatness. The NFL record book does it for them."

By contrast, the Eagles realized that they had not done quite enough to win. "I was proud of the effort and they battled," coach Andy Reid told The Associated Press, "but we came up just short—too many turnovers—and against such a tough football team you can't do that."

It was not for lack of trying. McNabb had made every effort to win. The Eagles' quarterback passed for 357 yards and three touchdowns. But he was intercepted three times and sacked four times by the Patriots. New England also "kept him from scrambling" and gaining yards on the ground, according to *Florida Times-Union* reporter Vito Stellino.

A report in *The New York Times* claimed that McNabb might have been sick in the last quarter. Reporter Frank Litsky said that the Super Bowl "was winding down in the last 5 minutes 40 seconds, and Philadelphia was trying to close a 10-point deficit against the New England Patriots, but the

Donovan McNabb is shown late in the fourth quarter of Super Bowl XXXIX as the Eagles tried to make a comeback against the New England Patriots. Philadelphia's efforts fell short, 24-21, and one of McNabb's teammates said that the quarterback fell ill during the Eagles' final drives.

Eagles seemed overly casual." Eagles **center** Hank Fraley suggested that McNabb was sick. "He could hardly call the plays," Fraley said. "That's how exhausted he was trying to give it his all. ... He was puking at the time, trying to hold it in."

But McNabb disagreed. "No, I wasn't sick, and no, I didn't throw up," he said, according to *The New York Times*. "If people want to use that as an excuse for why we lost, that's not the way it was, but I'll put it on my shoulders."

As Bob Brookover of *The Philadelphia Inquirer* put it, "The Eagles had their moments in Super Bowl XXXIX. They just didn't have the final one when NFL officials wheeled out the victory platform and presented the Vince Lombardi Trophy" to the Super Bowl champion.

As McNabb said, "When you're trying to make every play possible, you have to dig deep. We were just trying to give it all we had."

In fact, this sentence might sum up Donovan McNabb's entire career.

A Childhood
in Illinois

Donovan Jamal McNabb was born on November 25, 1976. He was the second child of Sam and Wilma McNabb, who had a four-year-old boy named Sean. The McNabb family lived in Chicago, Illinois, on the southern shore of Lake Michigan. With a population of about 3 million people, Chicago was the biggest city in the Midwest. Donovan's father, Sam McNabb, was an electrical engineer for a local company while his mother, Wilma, was a pediatric nurse. They met at Morgan Park High School and married soon after graduation.

TWO CONCERNED PARENTS
When Donovan and Sean were small children, their parents devoted as much time as possible to instilling strong values

in the two boys. Sam served as a powerful role model for his sons. He had learned how to be an effective parent from his own mother and father—Alfred and Marenda McNabb. "They were the people I looked to and pulled from for strength, discipline, and guidance as I grew from childhood to manhood," he told D.A. Sears, managing editor of *In Search of Fatherhood.* "I think as children, we learn to believe and confide in our parents if they are consistent in their approach to parenting," he continued. Sam McNabb said that he also "looked up to"

THE SOUTH SIDE OF CHICAGO

The McNabbs lived on the South Side of Chicago—an area that is rich in history. The lyrics to a popular song—"On the South Side of Chicago"—went this way:

New Orleans was groovy, Memphis light and gay
And who could put down New York's Broadway
But there was everything on the South Side of Chicago.

During the nineteenth century, Chicago became a flourishing port on the Great Lakes and a busy railroad hub for the expanding Midwest. The city's South Side became the home of the sprawling Illinois Steel Company and the Union Stock Yard. The Stock Yard supplied beef to Chicago's successful meat-packing plants, which shipped meat to towns and cities across the United States. The Pullman Palace Car Company also built its luxury railroad cars on the South Side. By the latter part of the nineteenth century, millions of immigrants were coming to the United States from Europe, and many of them traveled to the South Side to work in the stockyards and steel mills. They included Irish, Germans, Czechs, and East European Jews.

Dr. Martin Luther King, Jr., the great civil-rights leader "for his strength and courage."

Among the qualities that Sam McNabb taught his sons were "how to be respectful," and to "eliminate selfishness and instill humility." As he emphasized, "Everything should start at home and we know they [our two sons] have bought into our method of parenting." Sam recalled that, after his sons were born, he talked to his own father and sought his advice on how to be an effective parent. His father would "give you a certain

By the early twentieth century, a large number of African Americans were leaving the South for northern cities like Chicago. They were escaping from years of poverty and racial discrimination, hoping to find better lives in places like the South Side. They brought jazz music with them from Memphis and New Orleans. Many also found higher-paying jobs on the South Side, but they encountered racial prejudice there, too.

In 1919, a race riot broke out in Chicago, leading to 38 deaths, mostly on the South Side. Whites began to move to the suburbs, leaving African Americans behind. During the last half of the twentieth century, the South Side's manufacturing plants and meat-packing companies also shut their doors—moving to other cities where the cost of doing business was cheaper. As the South Side declined, African Americans who could afford to move out were migrating to the Chicago suburbs, where it was safer to live. Eventually, Sam and Wilma McNabb decided to move their family out to the suburbs, too.

After several years of doing Campbell's Chunky Soup commercials together, Donovan McNabb and his mother, Wilma, were joined in the ads in 2005 by Donovan's father, Sam. As parents, Wilma and Sam McNabb strove to instill strong values in their sons, Donovan and Sean, as the two were growing up.

look to convince you it was better to accept his decision rather than challenge him. Very seldom did he ever have to repeat himself when we were to do something."

Sam said he also learned a great deal from his father-in-law, Wilma's father. He taught Sam how to be more "understanding" in his approach to parenting. As Sam told Sears, "He would never tell me that I made a mistake or when I used poor judgment in some of my decisions. He would always say how important it was to be more flexible and less rigid in making decisions by listening to your children and learning how to communicate with them as opposed to always dictating to them."

Sam McNabb believes that there are certain tools that parents should give their children to enable them to become self-fulfilled adults. He said that it is important for them to learn that "no one is going to hand them anything without a good effort." They must also learn to be "sturdy, strong, considerate, and well-grounded." A third essential tool is "to make sure that children always keep their balance in making good decisions, being obedient, and choosing good friends or peers."

Donovan's mother, Wilma, also played a crucial role in his upbringing. According to the Web site JockBio.com, "she spent countless hours talking with her children and helping them work through whatever problems they faced." Donovan remembered that his mother was a strict disciplinarian. As he told sports columnist Michael Wilbon of *The Washington Post*, "She'd pop you in the back of your head if you did something wrong." Wilma agreed. "'Popped' is probably a pretty good way of describing it. With a fist. Is old-school a fair way of describing my philosophy on raising children? Oh, yes, it is. It's fair."

In an interview with Harry Smith on *The Early Show* on CBS, Wilma McNabb was asked if she guessed that Donovan might be a superstar one day when he was still a young boy. "Not at all," she answered. "You just want your children to grow up to be successful college graduates and go on to make their own way in life. But he chose sports, and that was a good thing. It kept him busy and kept him focused and in his books."

MOVING TO THE SUBURBS

When Donovan was eight years old, his parents had decided to do what other residents of the South Side had done—move out of Chicago to the suburbs. They hoped to provide their sons with a better education and a safer environment in which to grow up. The McNabb family moved to Dolton, Illinois, just south of Chicago. At first, Dolton turned out to be far different from what they had expected. As the first African Americans in the neighborhood, Donovan and his family were not warmly greeted by the whites who lived there. In fact, their house was attacked by vandals who broke windows and painted graffiti on the walls.

In the mid-1980s, there was still strong racial prejudice in the United States. Some white families who had left the cities for the suburbs did not want African Americans moving into suburban neighborhoods. But Sam and Wilma McNabb were strong enough to handle the intolerance that they encountered in Dolton. Gradually, they even succeeded in breaking down some of this prejudice and made friends with a few of the neighbors.

In school, Donovan also began to make a place for himself. With a warm personality and a natural sense of humor, he was successful in charming students and teachers alike. Meanwhile, his brother, Sean, was making a name as a star football and basketball player. According to JockBio.com, "Donovan idolized Sean. He hung out at his practices, watched all his games, and even served as manager of one of his hoops [basketball] teams." In elementary school, Donovan did not participate in any sport himself; in fact, he did not seem to take sports too seriously. This outlook changed in junior high school. Following in his brother's footsteps, Donovan wanted to play in one of the football leagues for kids.

During the 1930s, youth football leagues had begun to develop in Philadelphia, Pennsylvania. They were originally organized by a stockbroker named Joseph Tomlin. Tomlin had been asked to set up several teams by local factory owners. The windows on their factories were regularly being broken by local kids, and they wanted to stop it. Tomlin persuaded the factory owners to sponsor a football league to keep the kids occupied.

At first, the league had only four teams, but it gradually expanded to 16 teams. In 1933, Tomlin asked Glenn Scobie "Pop" Warner, a legendary college football coach, to speak at an early spring meeting of his young players. On April 19, 1934, Warner traveled through high winds and snow to attend the conference. His speech electrified the young players and at the end of the evening, "by popular acclaim," the fledging youth program was renamed the Pop Warner Conference, according to the Pop Warner Little Scholars Web site. Leagues spread across the United States, and by the 1970s, more than 3,000 teams existed, involving hundreds of thousands of young people.

One of them was Donovan McNabb. Since Donovan was smaller than his brother, his mother was afraid that he might get severely hurt in tackle football. The local coach, though, convinced her that he should play. He started at quarterback, a position that he continued to play throughout his career. "At that age," he told authors John Horn and Jennifer York, "you try to use a lot of … moves because you don't want to be hit as a young child, playing football for the first time. You watched so many big hits on TV, you don't want to be one of them. You make a lot of moves and see if you can avoid some people. [You] try to limit it to as few hits as you can."

SUCCESS AT MT. CARMEL HIGH SCHOOL

In 1990, Donovan took his enthusiasm for football to Mt. Carmel High School. Mt. Carmel is on Chicago's South Side, close to the shores of Lake Michigan. The all-boys Catholic school was founded in 1900 as part of St. Cyril College. Established by the Carmelite order of Catholic brothers and priests, it included a program for junior high and high school students, a four-year college, and a vocational school. In 1924, a new building, which would be Mt. Carmel High School, was constructed on the campus. Mt. Carmel is an outstanding private school that sends most of its students onto four-year colleges. It also boasts one of the city's premier athletic programs. Beginning in the 1920s, the football team won a series of citywide championships. After the school decided to participate in state tournaments, the football team went on to win nine titles during the 1980s and 1990s under its legendary

Frank Lenti, the head football coach at Mt. Carmel High School in Chicago, sits with four of the nine state championship trophies his teams have won. Lenti named Donovan McNabb as his starting quarterback in 1992, Donovan's junior year.

coach Frank Lenti. The school also fielded a nationally known basketball team.

Mt. Carmel seemed to be a natural choice for both Sean and Donovan McNabb. After entering the ninth grade in 1990, Donovan immediately began to make a name for himself in football and basketball. In 1992, Coach Lenti selected McNabb as his starting quarterback. Lenti used the pro-**option** offense, which required a quarterback who could think quickly and demonstrate a variety of athletic skills. This attack only "works well with a quarterback that can run the ball like a running back," according to the *Football Playbook*. "The option allows for flexibility and the ability of the quarterback to control the running attack—the quarterback can hand off to the **fullback** for a dive, turn the ball upfield for the end sweep, or pitch it out to the halfback. ... The quarterback must be able to read the defense and decide when to pitch or keep it upfield."

Donovan possessed all the gifts necessary to run the option offense. In practice sessions, he was so wily that he ran the defensive players ragged. One of Donovan's teammates was defensive end Simeon Rice, who was drafted by the Arizona Cardinals of the National Football League in 1996. "He got so frustrated chasing Donovan around the practice field," according to JockBio.com, "that he sometimes buried [tackled] him after the whistle had blown."

Donovan proved that he was a masterful quarterback. And he needed to be because Mt. Carmel expected him to win games. As assistant coach Wally Sebuck told *Philadelphia Inquirer* reporter Anthony Gargano, "At Carmel, you're expected to perform. You're expected to be a man and rise above the normal thing you'd expect from a kid, from a teenager. Out of a class of 200 freshmen, 150 will go out for football. And you'd better keep up your grades. You can't just be at Carmel, you have to be part of it. Donovan was the starting quarterback at Carmel. This should tell you a little about the kid's makeup."

Besides football, Donovan was also a member of the Mt. Carmel basketball team. He played point guard—the man who directs the offense. One starter on the team was Antoine Walker, who later played for coach Rick Pitino at the University of Kentucky. Afterward, Walker was drafted to play for the Boston Celtics in the National Basketball Association.

When Donovan was a senior, the Mt. Carmel basketball team went 25–4. And Donovan was named an all-area player by the *Chicago Sun-Times* newspaper.

Indeed, Donovan was such as standout at Mt. Carmel that he was heavily recruited by a number of leading college athletic programs. The University of Nebraska football team, coached by Tom Osborne, wanted him. And he was also recruited by Syracuse University. In the end, McNabb turned down

Nebraska because he might have to spend two years playing backup to another quarterback, Tommie Frazier.

He decided instead to attend Syracuse. Coach Paul Pasqualoni was looking for a starting quarterback. In addition, Donovan would be given an opportunity to play for the Syracuse basketball team, coached by one of the National Collegiate Athletic Association's (NCAA) finest coaches, Jim Boeheim. Finally, Syracuse had one of the nation's leading communications schools. While playing two sports, Donovan also hoped to get the type of communications training that might one day make him a successful sportscaster after he retired from the gridiron.

Success at Syracuse

Donovan McNabb started his career at Syracuse during the summer of 1994, but he did not begin to play football immediately. Instead, coach Paul Pasqualoni decided to red-shirt him. That is, he wanted to give McNabb a year to practice, watch the team, and learn the plays before actually competing on the gridiron. "I learned how to watch film, how to evaluate defenses," McNabb told *New York Times* reporter William Wallace.

By the start of the 1995 football campaign, McNabb finally seemed to have the seasoning that he needed. Still, he had no guarantee that he would start as quarterback. He was competing for the starting position against two other talented players—Kevin Johnson and Keith Downing. But on the day of the opening game against the University of North Carolina,

Pasqualoni selected McNabb as his **starter**. "I prepared myself not to make mistakes," he told Wallace later, "to try to make the right decisions and win the game."

During the first three quarters, the opening game remained very close, with North Carolina clinging to a slim lead. Then in the last quarter, McNabb put together three successful drives and the Orangemen won the game 20-9. It was a satisfying start to McNabb's career at Syracuse. Still, there would be ups and downs ahead in the season. In the next game, against East Carolina, Syracuse had built a commanding 21-0 lead partway through the second quarter. McNabb had engineered three successful drives in front of the hometown crowd of almost 40,000 fans at the Carrier Dome.

Then East Carolina came roaring back. Its quarterback, Marcus Crandell, reeled off four touchdown passes during the rest of the game to lead East Carolina to a 27-24 win. "I can't remember us being up by 21-0 and losing a game," Coach Pasqualoni told *New York Times* reporter Frank Litsky. But that is what happened. While McNabb had completed 11 of 23 passes for 231 yards and had run for 80 yards, Crandell surpassed him by passing for 392 yards. "We let it slip away," Pasqualoni told Litsky afterward. And McNabb added: "I guess it's something you have to learn from."

And McNabb did learn. He guided the Orangemen to victory in their next eight games. As offensive coordinator George DeLeone told William Wallace of *The New York Times,* "The big thing Donovan has done for us is being careful with the football. Coaches expect freshmen to do things that can hurt you. Don hasn't forced passes, hasn't hurt us with turnovers, and has been able to make good decisions. That's his biggest plus. Second, he has the unique ability to make plays, **scrambles** at the appropriate time. When a play breaks down, he can find people downfield. That's a knack, a real gift."

One of his favorite targets was wide receiver Marvin Harrison. Averaging more than 20 yards each time he caught the ball, he gained more than 1,000 yards during the season. In fact, Harrison went on to be a top pick in the National Football League **draft** after the 1995 season.

Bringing an outstanding record into the final game of the season, McNabb, Harrison, and their teammates faced Miami. Although Syracuse rolled up a 10-point lead in the first half, the Orangemen lost the game 35-24, ending their season at 9–2. McNabb was named Rookie of the Year in the Big East Conference.

In the postseason, Syracuse faced Clemson in the Gator Bowl. McNabb got off to a quick start in the first quarter, completing 85 percent of his passes and leading Syracuse to a 20-0 lead. "It came so easy to us, especially in the first quarter," said Syracuse guard Cy Ellsworth, according to Associated Press reporter Pete Iacobelli. "It broke their spirits, you could see it in their eyes and, in my opinion, they gave up." Harrison had two touchdown receptions from McNabb, who also ran for a touchdown. "All season long I continued to get better, and we put it all together in the bowl game," McNabb said after the game, according to Iacobelli. The Orangemen pasted Clemson, 41-0, for the most lopsided bowl victory in school history.

THE CAMPAIGN CONTINUES

After the 1995 football season ended, McNabb began to play basketball for Syracuse coach Jim Boeheim. Most of his time, however, was spent on the bench. Nevertheless, he participated in one of the school's great seasons, as Syracuse went to the NCAA championship game against Kentucky. Unfortunately, Syracuse lost to a University of Kentucky team led by Antoine Walker, a classmate of McNabb's from Mt. Carmel.

A few months later, McNabb began his second season as Syracuse quarterback. Unfortunately, he got off to a poor start with defeats at the hands of North Carolina and Minnesota. Then the Orangemen started to turn the season around with a 52-21 win over the Virginia Tech Hokies. Behind McNabb's

Syracuse quarterback Donovan McNabb followed through on a pass during the second quarter of the Gator Bowl against Clemson, held on January 1, 1996. Syracuse won the game 41-0, as McNabb passed for three touchdowns. He was named the most valuable player of the game.

leadership, Syracuse had a 24-14 lead at halftime. In the third quarter, Virginia Tech pulled within three points, 24-21. At this point, McNabb went into high gear, completing a scoring pass that lengthened the lead to 31-21. On this play he managed to scramble away from the defenders and complete a pass to Quinton Spotwood in the end zone. After that score, Syracuse never looked back, scoring three more touchdowns and ending a 13-game Virginia Tech winning streak. McNabb had an outstanding day with 123 yards in the air and 162 yards on the ground.

Pasqualoni was very pleased with McNabb's progress at Syracuse. As he told *New York Times* reporter William C. Rhoden, "He's what college football's all about. Great kid. Humble. Polite. Isn't bigger than the game. Isn't bigger than his team." Pasqualoni, though, was under no illusion that Syracuse could repeat its 1995 performance. "We are not taking for granted that because Donovan McNabb had a good year last year that automatically it is his birthright to have a great season this year," he explained to Rhoden.

Samuel and Wilma McNabb also tried to make sure that all the attention Donovan received during the 1995 season did not affect his performance. "I would call him periodically just to see where he was," Samuel McNabb told Rhoden. "I wanted to make sure that I didn't have to come over there to Syracuse and start bursting egos. Fortunately, I didn't have to do that: He was very focused on what he wanted to do."

Part of what Donovan wanted to accomplish, according to Rhoden, was "to become as highly rated by professional teams by his senior year as he is regarded now by college rivals. ... The questions facing Donovan McNabb are more immediate: Will he duplicate or surpass last season's performance? Will he drop off? Will he be as focused?" Pasqualoni had complete confidence in him. "He has old-fashioned values," the coach said. "Donovan McNabb knows the meaning of having a work ethic."

McNabb proved it in the win over Virginia Tech. Although, according to *New York Times* writer William Wallace, he was making offensive coordinator George DeLeone a bit nervous. When McNabb was running the option play, DeLeone got "very upset. He takes one hand off the football. I don't want him to do it." But, according to Wallace, "McNabb said he has been carrying it like that since high school and that he is not about to stop. The defending cornerback is almost certain to take the fake and then watch McNabb fly by, running free into the **secondary**."

Using this approach, McNabb had gained 72 yards against the Hokies on a single play. And his success continued during the rest of the season, as Syracuse won eight games in a row. McNabb led the team to a victory over Rutgers, 42-0, as he threw for one touchdown and scored another one on the ground. That first touchdown came on a pass to Roland Williams, after McNabb had faked a run in the opposite direction. Later in the season, McNabb led the Orangemen to a victory over Boston College, 45-17, as he passed for 328 yards.

In 1996, McNabb was named Big East Offensive Player of the Year, but he could not manage to defeat archrival Miami, which won a close 38-31 game at the end of the season. Nevertheless, Syracuse received a bid to the Liberty Bowl, where they beat Houston 30-17.

1997 SEASON

The Liberty Bowl win probably provided some momentum for McNabb and his team as they began the 1997 season. Late in August, Syracuse met Wisconsin in front of more than 51,000 fans at Giants Stadium in New Jersey. Wideout Kevin Johnson of Syracuse got the game started right by returning the opening kickoff 89 yards for a touchdown. McNabb took over from there. As *Philadelphia Inquirer* reporter Ray Parrillo wrote, "The 6-foot-3, 219-pound junior paralyzed the [Wisconsin] Badgers with his quick feet and burned them with laser passes." In the second quarter, McNabb scored on his own 21-yard run, and later, McNabb completed a pass to Syracuse tight end Kaseem Sinceno for a touchdown. Meanwhile, the Syracuse defense did not allow Wisconsin into the end zone. The final score was 34-0.

Commenting on McNabb's performance to Parrillo, Wisconsin coach Barry Alvarez said, "He can make things happen. He caused a lot of problems for our defense."

"I felt great," McNabb said after the game, according to Parrillo. "I want to be a good leader, make plays, and set the tone for the team. I think this was a game to let people know about Syracuse football, to show how good we can be, because we know how good we can be."

Syracuse, though, was not as good as McNabb thought. Following the Wisconsin victory, the team lost the next three games, to North Carolina State, Oklahoma, and Virginia Tech. The Hokies defeated Syracuse 31-3, as McNabb only passed for 198 yards and seemed stymied by the Virginia Tech defense. If Syracuse hoped to advance to another bowl game at the end of the season, the Orangemen would need to reel off a string of victories.

And that's exactly what Syracuse did. In early October, the Orangemen beat East Carolina 56-0. McNabb ran for a couple of touchdowns and passed for a third one to Quinton Spotwood. In late November, Syracuse faced rival Miami once again. The Big East title was on the line, and the Orangemen did not disappoint their fans, winning 33-13. The victory was Syracuse's first over Miami in seven tries in the 1990s. McNabb passed for one touchdown to wide receiver Jim Turner, followed by another pass for 49 yards to Turner and a second score. Then McNabb engineered a third touchdown drive, with rushes of 29 and 11 yards, before the first half ended. "Fiesta Bowl, here we come!" said Syracuse safety Jamont Kinds after the game, according to *New York Times* reporter Charlie Nobles.

The Fiesta Bowl on December 31, 1997, proved to be another blowout. This time, however, Syracuse was on the losing end, 35-18, to the Kansas State Wildcats. In fact, the Wildcats had run up a 21-3 lead in the second quarter. Later in the game, Syracuse pulled to within 28-18, but McNabb **fumbled** the ball on the Kansas State 14-yard line. Nevertheless, he managed to run for 81 yards during the game, more than any other offensive player on the field.

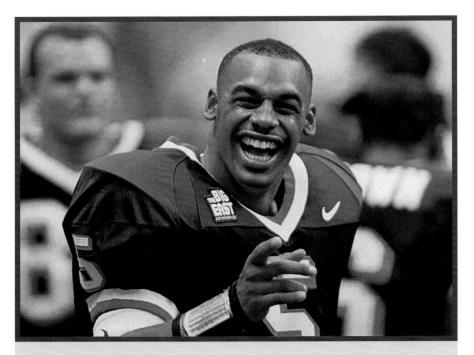

A happy Donovan McNabb cheered on the second-string players during Syracuse's lop-sided 56-0 win over East Carolina during the 1997 season. McNabb led the Orangemen to the Big East Conference title that year.

CLOSING A CAREER AT SYRACUSE

After the 1997 season, McNabb decided not to play basketball for Syracuse any longer. Instead he devoted himself to extra physical training and reviewed films from the previous year's football games. He hoped that this additional work might result in the best season ever for the Orangemen in 1998. McNabb also wanted to put the loss in the Fiesta Bowl behind him. "Syracuse trailed early but was coming back when McNabb fumbled inside the [Kansas State] Wildcats' 15-yard line and sealed the defeat," wrote William Rhoden of *The New York Times*. "That play haunted McNabb all winter, spring and summer."

"It's been a hungry summer," he told Rhoden. "I'm out on a mission. I'm out to quiet critics of what Donovan McNabb and the Syracuse Orangemen are not capable of doing. We're out to prove a point."

McNabb wanted to bring Syracuse to the level of the top college teams in the United States—programs like Penn State and Florida. Instead, the 1997 season had been a series of ups and downs with one big loss at the end. "All we have to do is win some big out-of-conference games," McNabb pointed out to Rhoden. "It's like you're wearing the same gym shoes," he added. "You continuously wear the same gym shoes, then you wear them again, then the next year you're wearing the same shoes. You want more. With the team that we have this year, we feel that 9–3, 9–4 is not a successful season."

But the season began with an agonizing loss to Tennessee in early September in front of a home crowd of almost 50,000 fans. McNabb had an outstanding game with 298 yards passing and two touchdowns. He also scored another touchdown on the ground, and Syracuse had the lead with about two minutes left to play. But a **pass interference** call on a Syracuse defender helped spark a last-minute Tennessee drive. With very little time remaining, Tennessee kicker Jeff Hall made a 27-yard field goal and Syracuse suffered a devastating 34-33 loss.

The following week was much better as Syracuse defeated Michigan 38-28. The season, though, seemed again to go up and down from there, with losses to North Carolina State in the fourth game and West Virginia in the eighth game. Along the way, the Orangemen managed to beat Rutgers in a lopsided 70-14 game. During the game, McNabb reached a milestone— setting a Big East record for most career touchdown passes at 61.

In mid-October, McNabb led his team to a 42-25 victory over rival Boston College. He not only passed for 182 yards and two touchdowns but also carried the ball 11 times. As Boston College coach Tom O'Brien told Jack Cavanaugh of *The New York Times,* "He gets out of situations that are unbelievable. I don't think he misthrew a pass in the first half. The guy's a magician." By the end of the half, Syracuse had run

Donovan McNabb scrambled past Miami defender Dan Morgan *(right)* during the first quarter of their 1998 showdown at the Carrier Dome in Syracuse. The Orangemen shellacked Miami 66-13 to capture another Big East title. McNabb scored three touchdowns on the ground and passed for two more.

up a 21-3 lead and doubled their point score in the second half. On one of these scoring drives, McNabb threw the ball past three defenders to complete a touchdown pass to wide receiver Jeff Lowe.

Syracuse went on to win the Big East title with a lopsided victory over Miami, 66-13. In that game, McNabb scored three touchdowns on the ground and made two scoring passes to his receivers. This was his last regular-season game as a member of the Syracuse team. And the fans at the Carrier Dome recognized his unmatched accomplishments with repeated standing ovations.

"I don't know if the fans could have cheered any longer or any harder for one guy," coach Paul Pasqualoni told reporter Charlie Nobles of *The New York Times*. "He is as well-loved a kid in the community as any we've had. He's been a role model for every kid in New York." Other coaches, like Florida State's Bobby Bowden and Florida's Steve Spurrier, also praised McNabb, who was named Big East Offensive Player of the Year for the third season in a row. "He can escape people," Spurrier told Nobles. "You can hardly **tackle** him, you can't sack him, and he's an excellent passer." Bowden, according to Nobles, "calls Donovan McNabb the country's best college football player."

Unfortunately, all of this praise did not help Syracuse or McNabb in the Orange Bowl in early January 1999. Spurrier's Florida Gators overwhelmed Syracuse 31-10. The Gators managed to shut down McNabb, who fumbled the football twice

DONOVAN McNABB'S SYRACUSE STATISTICS

Following are Donovan McNabb's passing statistics for his four seasons as quarterback at Syracuse University. He also rushed for 1,561 yards and 19 touchdowns during his college career.

YEAR	COMP	ATT	PCT	YD	TD
1995	128	207	61.8	1,991	16
1996	118	215	54.9	1,776	19
1997	145	265	54.7	2,448	20
1998	157	251	62.5	2,134	22
Career	548	938	58.4	8,349	77

and threw an interception. Syracuse offensive coordinator Kevin Rogers told Nobles that McNabb was "off his mark," in the Orange Bowl game. It was a depressing end to a very successful Syracuse career. "Mainly, what I'll remember is the close friendships I've made, friendships I'll have for the rest of my life," McNabb added. "It's going to be hard sitting back on Saturdays and watching a team I was part of for five years."

McNabb was also part of the Syracuse basketball team, at least for three seasons. "He's a great teammate," coach Jim Boeheim told Pete Thamel of *The New York Times*. "He played hard in practice and pushed guys. He fit in right away, led the team in cheers on the bench. He was a tremendous teammate."

McNabb would continue to demonstrate his unique talents on and off the field in the years ahead.

McNabb Enters the Pros

"**D**onovan McNabb has had a very good week," Oakland Raiders coach Jon Gruden told *The New York Times*. "He has answered any questions people may have about his ability." Gruden was coaching the North squad in the 1999 Senior Bowl. The annual Senior Bowl brought together the best senior athletes in football for one final contest in their college careers. This game was McNabb's last stop before entering the pros. Although the North eventually lost the game to the South squad, McNabb was one of the stars. As Jacksonville Jaguars coach Tom Coughlin added, "He showed he had great arm strength to go along with the mobility everyone knew about." McNabb had proven that he was worthy to be selected in one of the early rounds of the National Football League Draft.

The NFL Draft was held in April in New York City. Professional football teams chose from a group of outstanding players, mostly college juniors and seniors. Traditionally, the teams with the worst records from the previous season were given the first picks in each of seven rounds, so they could choose the top collegiate stars. Because the Philadelphia Eagles had won only three games in the 1998 season, they had the second selection in the first round of the 1999 draft.

Many Philadelphia fans wanted the Eagles to select running back Ricky Williams from the University of Texas. Williams had received the **Heisman Trophy**, the most prestigious award in college football, given annually to the sport's top performing player. But the Eagles' new coach, Andy Reid, was very impressed with McNabb. He had been a highly successful option quarterback at Syracuse and a standout in the Senior Bowl. Reid also thought that McNabb had what it took to learn the very demanding **West Coast offense**, which the Eagles planned to use in the season ahead.

The West Coast offense had been popularized by coach Bill Walsh of the San Francisco 49ers during the 1980s. The offense relied on a highly agile quarterback to make quick, short passes from the outset of a game. The purpose was to spread the defense and open up lanes for pass receivers. Once the defense had been spread out, these lanes could also be used by the offense to execute running plays for long yardage. The West Coast offense, though, was complex and difficult to learn, requiring a highly intelligent, mobile quarterback.

As far as Reid was concerned, McNabb fit the bill perfectly. So the Eagles decided to bypass Williams and select McNabb as their first-round draft choice. This decision was not popular with many Philadelphia fans. In fact, some of them who attended the draft booed McNabb when he was chosen over Williams. Nevertheless, McNabb became one of only a handful of African-American quarterbacks who had ever received an opportunity to play in the NFL. One of the others had been

Family and friends surrounded Donovan McNabb after he was selected by the Philadelphia Eagles with the No. 2 pick in the 1999 NFL Draft. Some Philadelphia fans were not pleased that the team had chosen McNabb and booed him at the draft.

Randall Cunningham, who had played for Philadelphia from 1985 to 1995.

In response to his selection in the draft, McNabb told Phil Sheridan of *The Philadelphia Inquirer*, "A lot of people have aspirations to play on this level, but some have been stigmatized because of their skin color. Now we've opened the door to give them more confidence that if they work hard, they will have an opportunity." Only three black quarterbacks had been selected in the first round of the draft before McNabb. They were Doug Williams, chosen by the Tampa Bay Buccaneers in 1978; Andre Ware, taken by the Detroit Lions in 1990; and Steve McNair, selected by the Houston Oilers in 1995.

Frank Lenti, who had coached McNabb at Mt. Carmel High School, was not surprised by McNabb's selection. "When he left here," Lenti told Sheridan, "we had coaches betting each other whether he would win the Heisman Trophy before he was done." In the past, African Americans who had played quarterback in high school were regularly moved to other positions by college coaches. The University of Illinois had been interested in McNabb, but the school's offensive coordinator, Greg Landry, wanted him to be a wide receiver. "Coach, I

RICKY WILLIAMS

You would be hard-pressed to find an Eagles fan today who still wishes the team had chosen Ricky Williams instead of Donovan McNabb. After the Eagles took McNabb with the second pick in the 1999 draft, the New Orleans Saints chose Williams with the fifth pick. The Saints had traded all of their draft picks as well as two 2000 picks in order to move up to draft Williams.

He played three seasons with the Saints, rushing for 884 yards in his rookie season, 1,000 yards in his second season, and 1,245 yards in his third year. Still, despite his above-average numbers, the Saints traded Williams in 2002 to the Miami Dolphins in exchange for two first-round draft picks. In his first year with the Dolphins, Williams led the league in rushing with 1,853 yards. He had another good year the following season, with 1,372 rushing yards.

In May 2004, it was announced that Williams had tested positive for marijuana use and would be suspended for four games. Then, just before training camp was scheduled to begin, Williams abruptly announced that he was retiring from the don't recruit option quarterbacks," Landry explained to Lenti, according to Sheridan. "Donovan McNabb is not an option quarterback. He's a quarterback," Lenti replied. But Landry decided not to take him. "Two years later," Lenti said to Sheridan, "Donovan was taking Syracuse to bowl games, and Greg Landry was fired."

Kevin Rogers, the offensive coordinator at Syracuse University, also praised McNabb's abilities. Rogers remembered a time when he had called a specific play, but McNabb

sport. The Dolphins won only four games that season, and their coach was fired.

Williams returned to the Dolphins in July 2005, apologizing for leaving the team two days before training camp the year before. During his time away from the game, Williams traveled, studied holistic medicine, and became certified as a yoga instructor. He has said he does not regret his retirement decision and calls it the "most positive thing" he has ever done. In 2005, sharing time with running back Ronnie Brown, Williams played in 12 games and rushed for 743 yards.

In February 2006, the league announced that Williams had violated the NFL drug policy for a fourth time and would be suspended for the entire 2006 season. During his suspension, he played for the Toronto Argonauts of the Canadian Football League. The NFL reinstated Williams in November 2007, clearing him to play again for the Dolphins. In his first game back, he injured his pectoral muscle and missed the rest of the 2007 season. In that game, he rushed for 15 yards on six carries.

had decided to run a different play. "When Donovan came off the field," Rogers told Sheridan, "I asked him, 'What did you see?' He explained it, and I shook my head and told him, 'I don't think so.' The next day, I'm sitting in the film room [reviewing films of the game] and … he was right. He saw it, and I didn't."

But many Eagle fans were still upset that Reid had selected McNabb and let Ricky Williams get away to another team. So McNabb would have to prove himself in the months ahead. His father, Sam McNabb, had no doubt that he could do it. "Donovan is a big-hearted, warmhearted young man," McNabb told Sheridan of *The Philadelphia Inquirer*. "Once people in Philadelphia get to know him, they're going to embrace him."

PRESEASON AND A BIG CONTRACT

As McNabb attended his first day of an Eagles mini training camp in April 1999, he was asked how he felt. "I wanted to get started," he told Sheridan. "I wanted to show them [the team and the fans] that I can do what they want me to do. I just wanted to come out and do some things in the offense and try to stand out a little bit but continue to get better every time I step up." Reid had four quarterbacks at the camp—McNabb, Bobby Hoying, Koy Detmer, and Doug Pederson, whom Reid had brought in as the likely starter. One of them would be leading the Eagles' offense when the season began.

"He did a nice job today," Reid said, referring to McNabb. "We had a lot of [plays] in. That can be a little tricky, but he picked that up fine. It was just a handful of plays. We'll give him some more." For his part, McNabb was ready to be patient. He knew that Pederson was scheduled to start, but McNabb was also going to wait to see what might happen. "Patience is key," he said to Sheridan. "You can't rush anything, because you lose focus on what's at hand. I'm going to stay patient and learn from Doug Pederson because he's a veteran and he's been in the league for a number of years. … Coach Reid will make the decision. If it's me, I'll be very happy. If it's not, then I'll continue to work."

Meanwhile, McNabb's agent, Fletcher Smith, was busy negotiating a contract for the new Philadelphia quarterback. According to *The Philadelphia Inquirer,* he was reportedly asking for a seven-year deal worth close to $50 million with about $11 million as a **signing bonus**. By July, however, no contract had been signed and the negotiations had apparently hit a snag.

In comments to the press, Smith indicated that McNabb's race might be an issue. He was reportedly asking for a clause that would allow McNabb to become a free agent and get out of his contract after three or four seasons if his deal with the Eagles did not work out. Smith suggested that other quarterbacks—white quarterbacks—could command this type of contract. But it was being denied to McNabb—a black quarterback.

The Eagles were upset with Smith's statements because they had appointed African Americans to all the top jobs in their organization in the past. "Race will never be an issue, not now and not ever, from our side and in our approach," Reid said, according to Phil Sheridan. "We've put ourselves in a position to make this young man a very wealthy young man and at the same time give him an opportunity to be the best football player he possibly can be." By the end of July, the Eagles and McNabb finally had a deal. He had a contract that might be as high as $54 million, with bonuses, but the Eagles had refused to provide the other clauses that his agent wanted.

In August, McNabb was at training camp, and he worked out with the rest of the team in preparation for the 1999 season. The exhibition schedule, which each professional team plays before the start of the regular season, did not turn out to be successful for Philadelphia. With Pederson at the helm, the Eagles lost their first two preseason games—to the Baltimore Ravens, 10-7, and the New York Jets, 10-9. Meanwhile, McNabb experienced spasms in his back, but this problem apparently cleared up and he was ready to play.

After a loss to the Minnesota Vikings, Reid finally put McNabb into the final preseason game—against Cleveland. After replacing Pederson in the second half, McNabb made a series of short passes to score Philadelphia's first touchdown. This made the score 14-10 in favor of Cleveland. Then he added impressive runs and passes during the rest of the game, while the Eagle defense stopped Cleveland from reaching the end zone. In front of a crowd of 64,000 fans, McNabb threw three touchdown passes in a 30-17 win.

"It was fun to put points on the board," McNabb told reporter Phil Sheridan after the game. "We owe a lot of credit to our defense," he added.

THE FIRST SEASON

For Philadelphia, the 1999 season began about where the last season had ended. The first game resulted in a loss and in the second game—against the Tampa Bay Buccaneers—Pederson was injured. He had also had a poor performance, and Reid decided to replace him with McNabb in the second half. McNabb, though, had very little success against the Buccaneers' defense. He was sacked repeatedly and managed to throw for only 26 yards in a 19-5 loss.

Reid planned to start Pederson again the following week against the Buffalo Bills. He wanted to bring McNabb along slowly, let him learn as much as possible by watching the team play, and then—if Pederson did not improve—make McNabb the starter. The third game was no better than the others. The Eagles failed to score any points in a 26-0 loss to the Bills. By the following week, when Philadelphia lost to the New York Giants, Pederson realized that he might be permanently replaced. As he told reporter Anthony Gargano of *The Philadelphia Inquirer*, "Sometimes you have to swallow your pride and do what's best for your football team."

Donovan McNabb made his first NFL appearance during the second week of the 1999 season, after Doug Pederson was injured during a game against Tampa Bay. The Buccaneers' stifling defense made for quite an initiation. Here, McNabb is sacked during the game.

Reid, however, refused to abandon Pederson, and he brought the Eagles an upset victory against the Dallas Cowboys in early October. Although McNabb might have hoped to get the start, he remained concentrated. As he told Phil Sheridan of *The Philadelphia Inquirer,* "I try to stay focused on what's going on around here, continue to learn and make sure that, when the time comes, I'm ready." Reid was very impressed with McNabb's work ethic. "He's working very hard," Reid said. "He gets here early in the morning. He's conditioning himself every morning. Then he goes and grabs a little breakfast, then comes in and watches film before we ever meet. That's a real positive." Meanwhile Pederson had guided the team to two wins, and the Eagles seemed to be turning around their season.

The turnaround, though, did not last long, and Eagles fans who expected to see their team on a winning streak were disappointed. Philadelphia continued to suffer additional losses, including a 33-7 defeat at the hands of the Carolina Panthers in early November. "It was a debacle," Coach Reid told Phil Sheridan. "I've been talking about taking small steps forward and avoiding taking any steps backward. This was a step backward." McNabb played the second half of that game, but he was unable to accomplish much against the Panther defense. He could manage only a single touchdown drive and threw for just 68 yards. Philadelphia skidded to 2–7 for the season.

Finally, in the tenth week of the season, Reid decided to start McNabb in a game against the Washington Redskins. After Philadelphia spotted their opponents a 21-10 lead, McNabb brought the Eagles back in the second half, for only their third victory of the year. He completed 8 of 21 passes for 60 yards and rushed for 49 yards in the 35-28 win. The Philadelphia receivers dropped some of McNabb's passes, however, apparently because he threw much harder than Pederson. Although he had gotten off to a good start, McNabb was not

Donovan McNabb dove over the goal line for a touchdown in the third quarter of a game against the Washington Redskins on November 14, 1999. The game marked McNabb's first start as quarterback, and he led the team to a second-half comeback victory.

as impressive in the next game, which Philadelphia lost to the Indianapolis Colts 44-17. The Eagles turned the ball over five times on their way to defeat.

It was a different Philadelphia team that took the field against the Washington Redskins at the end of November. McNabb engineered two 91-yard touchdown drives, and the score was tied at the end of regulation play. Unfortunately, the Eagles lost in overtime, 20-17.

For McNabb, this first season was an important learning experience. He was becoming comfortable with his team, learning all the plays, and demonstrating—even in a losing season—that he had the ability to be a highly effective quarterback. Off the field, McNabb kept a low profile—staying out of the limelight and away from much media attention. He lived with his older brother, Sean, in Cherry Hill, New Jersey, outside of Philadelphia. While he could have afforded an expensive car, he chose instead to drive a much-lower-priced Chrysler. "It's a nice car," he told Anthony Gargano of *The Philadelphia Inquirer*. "I like it. One thing I don't like is when people talk about a person and talk about his money. I can't stand that. Just talk about the person and get to know that person, not what he has or how much money he can get." McNabb added: "People say, 'He's in the NFL, his head's going to blow up. He's a young guy. He doesn't know what he has.' Man, I know what I have. It's just I don't show people. I just take things in stride. … You won't see me in flashy cars or flashy clothes."

According to Gargano, McNabb "considers himself, regardless of how many times his name is printed or spoken, or the size of his contract, in no way a celebrity. 'See? I do the same things everybody else does. It's just you might see me on Sunday playing football.'"

McNabb continued playing on Sundays, but the Eagles also continued losing. In a loss to Dallas, McNabb suffered a left knee sprain. Still, he continued to practice and played the final game of the season—a 38-31 victory over the St. Louis Rams. McNabb threw three touchdown passes, including the game-winner. But for the Eagles, who finished at 5–11, it was definitely a season to forget. "That's over," McNabb told *The Philadelphia Inquirer*. "We need to look to the future now."

Achieving New Levels of Success

After the 1999 season ended, Donovan McNabb headed for warm, sunny Arizona. He spent a month at the home of his teammate and friend, wide receiver Charles Johnson, in Tempe. Each day they carried out a vigorous workout program that included weight lifting and running. "I was impressed with Donovan's work habits," Johnson told Phil Sheridan of *The Philadelphia Inquirer.* "He kept up with me. I'm an early riser, and he was right there. Of course, it helped that I jumped on his bed in the morning to wake him up."

McNabb added, "I was thinking about working out in New Orleans, but I knew Charles would be in Arizona. So I went there. We worked extremely hard. We have a feel for where each other will be, how he'll make his cuts [moves on the field], when the ball will come out." In March, McNabb was back in

Philadelphia along with Johnson to work out with the rest of the Eagles. McNabb had already been named the starting quarterback for the 2000 season.

"I wasn't ready last year," McNabb told Sheridan. "It just wasn't my time yet. You want to come in your first year and gain the respect of your teammates and try to improve. Your second year, you expect a lot more. I have to eliminate some of the mistakes I made last year and try to improve everywhere." As Marcus Hayes of the *Philadelphia Daily News* added, "It has been only a year, but the transformation among the Eagles is remarkable. Uncertainty has been replaced by confidence. … In no one is the change more dramatic than quarterback Donovan McNabb."

Both the Eagles and McNabb expected great things from themselves in the 2000 season. So did coach Andy Reid, who was impressed with the turnaround that seemed to have occurred on his team. He was especially impressed with McNabb, who had been his top draft choice a year earlier. As he said to Hayes, "The kid's getting better every day." McNabb himself had more confidence. During the off-season he had spoken to Indianapolis Colts quarterback Peyton Manning. And Manning had told McNabb that, in his second season, he would be a better quarterback who saw plays developing on the field more clearly and found the open receiver far more often.

By June, McNabb had been working with all the receivers, he had learned how to read defenses more effectively, and he knew how to deal with a **blitz** more successfully. This enabled him to scramble out of the pocket—where the quarterback stands just behind the line of scrimmage—or throw a pass before he was sacked. During training, McNabb had become the leader of the team. Now he seemed ready to lead the Eagles into the exhibition games and then the regular season.

LET THE GAMES BEGIN

In their first preseason game, the Eagles picked up about where they had left off at the end of 1999. They dropped a 33-22 game to the Cleveland Browns, although McNabb completed 10 of 13 passes, including a touchdown pass to running back Duce Staley. The second game was not much better, as Philadelphia lost to the Baltimore Ravens 16-13. Finally, McNabb and the Eagles turned their game around with a 34-32 victory over the Tennessee Titans, as McNabb threw for 163 yards and three touchdowns. The Eagles, though, finished the exhibition schedule with a loss at the hands of the Buffalo Bills. Nevertheless, McNabb had performed fairly well, and the Eagles seemed hopeful that 2000 would be an improvement over the previous season.

And it started that way, as the Eagles stunned the Dallas Cowboys with a 41-14 win in the first game. Behind McNabb's passing and Staley's rushing, Philadelphia had a 24-6 lead at halftime. At the beginning of the fourth quarter, McNabb ran for three yards to score a touchdown. Then he ran toward the goalposts, threw the ball over the crossbar, found Staley, and knocked him to the ground with a chest bump. Although the temperature reached 109°F (43°C), the playing conditions had apparently not bothered McNabb.

The victory over Dallas had strengthened the Eagles' confidence. But the following week, they suffered a big loss against the New York Giants, 33-18. Although McNabb passed for more than 200 yards and threw another touchdown in the game, he was sacked three times. McNabb's ability to scramble out of the pocket did not make up for poor pass protection from the Eagles' offensive line. As Jerry Brewer of *The Philadelphia Inquirer* put it, "The quarterback spent the first half scrambling because of bad pass protection and holding on to the ball too long. And there was miscommunication with the wide receivers."

The Eagles lost the next game to the Green Bay Packers, without scoring a touchdown. "I had a chance to watch Brett Favre [the Packers' quarterback]," McNabb told Marcus Hayes of the *Philadelphia Daily News*. "I watched him. I tried to learn some things." McNabb was sacked five times by the Green Bay defense and threw an interception.

The Eagles made up for the loss with an impressive 21-7 win against the New Orleans Saints, with McNabb throwing for two touchdowns. He completed 20 of 32 passes for 222 yards. "I never had a problem with losing my confidence," McNabb told *The New York Times*, referring to the two early losses. "For me to come out and play this way and lead my team to victory is important."

With a 2–2 record, the Eagles then went on to defeat the Atlanta Falcons, with McNabb passing for a career-high 311 yards. He was clearly getting better and better with each game. In the weeks that followed, the Eagles and McNabb scored victories against the Arizona Cardinals and the Chicago Bears. Suddenly Philadelphia had reached 5–3, winning as many games halfway through the season as the team had won in all of 1999.

In a return match against the New York Giants, though, the Eagles hit a bump in the road, letting themselves be over-whelmed in a dismal 24-7 loss on a cold, snowy afternoon. "I don't make any excuses," McNabb told reporter Steve Popper of *The New York Times*. "It's a little windy, a little snowy, but I have plays that are supposed to be made. I didn't make them. … You learn from it and you move forward." As Coach Reid put it, "I didn't think it was Donovan's best game, and it surely was not our receivers' best game. … I thought he was off, throwing behind receivers in some cases. Other times, they were dropped. I thought we were over it [dropping the ball]. Weather, wind, those are all excuses. … We've got to focus in and get it done." McNabb had passed for only one touchdown, to receiver Charles Johnson, in the loss.

Donovan McNabb soared over Eagles offensive guard Jermaine Mayberry and Redskins safety Mark Carrier in the second quarter of a game on November 26, 2000. McNabb's rush set up a field goal. After a few early-season setbacks, McNabb led the Eagles to an 11–5 record in his first full season as the starting quarterback.

Over the next few weeks, the Eagles bounced back with another win over Dallas. The Cowboys' quarterback, Randall Cunningham, had once been a standout with the Eagles. "He's a guy I idolized and watched throughout his career," McNabb told *The New York Times*. "I sort of want to be on the same page he was on." Not only was he passing like Cunningham, McNabb was also rolling up yards rushing. Averaging more than seven yards a carry, he was the leading rusher on the Eagles. And behind McNabb the Eagles kept winning, with victories over the Pittsburgh Steelers and the Arizona Cardinals propelling Philadelphia to the top of the NFC East with an 8–4 record. As Mike Freeman of *The New York Times* reported, "Donovan McNabb is a major force at quarterback."

In the game against the Steelers, McNabb brought the team back from behind for a thrilling 26-23 victory in overtime. With less than two minutes left in the game, McNabb completed a touchdown pass to running back Brian Mitchell, closing the gap to 23-20. After the Eagles recovered an onside kick, placekicker David Akers tied the game with a field goal as time was running out in regulation. Akers then scored the winning field goal in overtime.

In December, the Eagles defeated the Cleveland Browns 35-24 to make the National Football Conference playoffs. "We can say it now," Reid told *The New York Times*. "We had goals, the playoffs were one of them." The Eagles kept winning, finishing the season with a victory over the Cincinnati Bengals and an 11–5 record. It was a complete turnaround from the previous season.

THE PLAYOFFS

On a cold, blustery day in late December, the Eagles hosted the Tampa Bay Buccaneers in Philadelphia for the NFC **wild-card** game. In a lopsided contest, McNabb led the Eagles to a 21-3 victory, running for a touchdown and throwing for two more. While the Eagles protected McNabb in the pocket, he still had to scramble throughout the game to complete his passes. "I was enjoying myself," McNabb told Mike Freeman of *The New York Times*. Tampa Bay coach Tony Dungy added. "He did a great job today. He's made big plays all year. He really hurt us."

McNABB'S MEDIA MOMENTS

When Donovan McNabb had been chosen as the first-round draft pick in 1999, some Eagles fans had booed. Their attitude, though, changed as McNabb led Philadelphia to a winning season in 2000. Along the way, he had also become a radio and television personality in Philadelphia. McNabb had his own radio show on WXTU-FM, a country music station, as well as a weekly television show. McNabb had attended the S.I. Newhouse School of Public Communications at Syracuse University, where he learned how to perform in front of a microphone and on camera. On the air, McNabb's natural sense of humor usually came across on his shows. Asked about the referees after the Eagles had won a close game against the Washington Redskins, McNabb said: "I think the refs did an excellent job. I have to say that or they'll fine me. I like money so I think I'll just keep it," according to *Philadelphia Daily News* reporters Chris Brennan and Leon Taylor.

McNabb's sense of humor had also become well-known around the Eagles' locker room. During the 2000 season, coach Andy Reid recalled that he was approaching a team meeting when "I walked out into the hall, and I thought I heard my own voice," according to Michael Silver of *Sports Illustrated*. "I peeked in and saw Donovan imitating me cold, and he had the place in stitches. Then he saw me, and he just sat down and froze."

Derek Boyko, coordinator of media for the Eagles, also talked about McNabb's sense of humor. "I don't think the notoriety has affected him much at all," he told Brennan and Taylor. "He's the same guy, and he still has fun with this. He handles his job very well." As running back Duce Staley put it, "He's a young guy, but he's smart and positive. He's a leader."

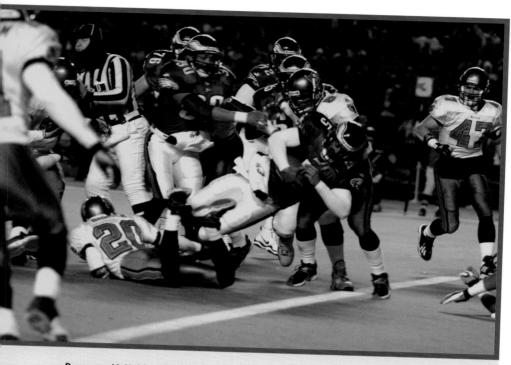

Donovan McNabb dove over the goal line to score the first touchdown in the Eagles' wild-card playoff game on December 31, 2000, against the Tampa Bay Buccaneers. The touchdown set the way for the Eagles, who won 21-3.

The victory over Tampa Bay set up a rematch with the New York Giants, who had beaten the Eagles twice earlier in the season. Previewing the game, reporter Harvey Araton of *The New York Times* wrote, "Twice this season, the Giants have put the Eagles right where they wanted them, flat on their backs. They had no problem containing McNabb, the second-year scrambler, who has accounted for three-quarters of the Eagles' offense." But the Giants defensive end Michael Strahan still had enormous respect for McNabb. "McNabb is a great player, a big problem, definitely the worst kind of quarterback you want to play against. You can rush the passer, but he may not be where you think he'll be."

The divisional playoff game, however, turned out to be a repeat of the earlier meetings between the Eagles and the Giants. New York sacked McNabb six times and beat Philadelphia 20-10. McNabb's first full season as starting quarterback had been very impressive, but the Eagles still had more left to accomplish.

After the season ended, McNabb was attending the Eagles' mini-camps. He was throwing hundreds of passes to receivers like James Thrash and Todd Pinkston, who were expected to be among the starters when the 2001 season began. He was also taping commercials and giving interviews to the press. Although McNabb had finished an outstanding year in 2000 and won the admiration of many Philadelphia fans, he had not put his initial introduction to the city behind him. McNabb still remembered the 1999 draft when he was booed by fans because the Eagles selected him instead of Ricky Williams.

"When I got booed at the draft," he told *New York Times* reporter Thomas George, "I looked over at my mom and she started to cry. I looked at my dad, and he was upset. My brother was mad. Me? Of course I took it personally. Now, I look at it as every opportunity I have to step on the field is a chance to show what I can do." In the same interview, McNabb added that he felt the media treated black quarterbacks differently. "I get tired of hearing about the mobility of black quarterbacks in the NFL. Hey, what about black quarterbacks being players who have done well in college, have been drafted and bring their knack of reading defenses, decision making, and leadership to the game? I just don't hear that part."

McNabb's father praised what his son had accomplished in Philadelphia. "There is nothing that Donovan starts that he does not feel he is capable of finishing as the very best," Sam McNabb said. Indeed, McNabb had rolled up almost 4,000 yards total, rushing and passing, in the 2000 season. With more than three-quarters of those yards in the air, he had matched the achievements of his hero Randall Cunningham,

CHUNKY SOUP

After the 2000 season, Donovan McNabb landed a new media job—spokesman for Campbell's Chunky Soup. "His potential is tremendous," Bob Williams, president of Burns Sports Celebrity Service, told *Philadelphia Inquirer* reporter Mike Bruton. Williams described McNabb as "charismatic and a handsome young athlete who plays the glamour position in football." Besides Chunky Soup, McNabb also had contracts with Nike and Verizon, the wireless communications company.

In the first Chunky commercials, McNabb appeared with Marcella Lowery, an actress who portrayed his mother. In one commercial, McNabb is supposed to be advertising a brand of shaving cream, when Lowery comes in to bring him some Chunky Soup. McNabb's parents came to the filming in Los Angeles, and Lowery said that having his mother there gave her some valuable insights into how to play his stage Mom for the commercials.

While attending the filming, Wilma McNabb realized that she had memorized all the lines and could play the part just as effectively. What's more, the commercials might be more true-to-life if McNabb's real mother played the part on television. She persuaded Campbell to take a chance on her. Wilma, whose middle name is Charlene, soon became known as "Star Char." Filming took about eight hours, and there were also news conferences and interviews. "I think what people see of me in the commercials is who I am. I'm just a big mom, someone who is very supportive," she told Michael Wilbon of *The Washington Post*. In 2005, Sam McNabb began to appear with his wife in the commercials.

who had also passed for more than 3,000 yards in a season as an Eagles quarterback.

A NEW SEASON

Before the new season began, Philadelphia suffered an exhibition loss to the Buffalo Bills followed by a 20-14 victory over the Tennessee Titans. With less than two minutes remaining in the first half, McNabb led the Eagles from their own 12-yard line to the Tennessee 2. Along the way, he completed passes to wide receivers Todd Pinkston and James Thrash and to running back Duce Staley. Then, McNabb dropped back into the pocket and completed another short throw to Thrash, giving the Eagles a 17-7 lead at halftime, big enough to win the game. McNabb passed for 117 yards, rushed for 94 yards, and had no interceptions.

Although the Eagles had a winning exhibition run, they opened the regular season with a 20-17 overtime loss to the St. Louis Rams. When McNabb fumbled on the opening **snap** from center at the Philadelphia 12-yard line, the Rams pounced on the ball and scored in two plays. A fumble in the second quarter led to another touchdown for the Rams. But McNabb led the Eagles in a comeback, completing a 98-yard drive with a pass to fullback Cecil Martin. After Martin scored another touchdown, the game was tied, before a field goal in overtime won it for the Rams.

Over the next few weeks, the Eagles bounced back. In a 27-3 victory over the Seattle Seahawks, McNabb threw two touchdown passes to Thrash and also scored a touchdown on a three-yard run. Then the Eagles pummeled the Dallas Cowboys 40-18, before losing a squeaker, 21-20, to the Arizona Cardinals. In that game, McNabb threw two touchdown passes to Pinkston. Once again, a McNabb fumble, as well as an interception, helped Arizona win the game.

But in one of the outstanding games of the early season, against the New York Giants, McNabb engineered a drive late in

As New York Giants defenders *(from left)* Mike Barrow, Michael Strahan, and Jason Sehorn flew at him, Donovan McNabb tried to dodge them late in a game on October 22, 2001, at Giants Stadium. With a fourth-quarter drive, McNabb led the Eagles to a come-from-behind 10-9 victory.

the game, scrambling away from defenders, completing passes, and finally capping the drive with an 18-yard pass to Thrash in the corner of the end zone for the winning touchdown. The 10-9 win was enough to propel the Eagles, at 3–2, to the top of the NFC East. After a loss the following week, Philadelphia took its revenge on Arizona with a convincing 21-7 victory. This time Thrash scored two touchdowns on passes from McNabb. In a 48-17 defeat of the Minnesota Vikings, McNabb electrified the crowd with his fancy footwork. On one drive he faked a pass and ran for 10 yards past the Viking defenders. He added another 15 yards after sidestepping Vikings' middle linebacker Kailee Wong. Finally, McNabb faked a **handoff** to running back Duce Staley, and ran the ball into the end zone from the Minnesota 12-yard line.

The Eagles then completed their third victory in a row by beating the Dallas Cowboys 36-3. "Each year stands alone," fullback Cecil Martin told reporter Phil Sheridan after the game. By early December, Philadelphia had a record of 7–4 and was two games ahead in the NFC East. Two weeks later, the Eagles had improved their record to 9–4 with victories over San Diego and Washington. In the victory over the Redskins, McNabb completed a 62-yard pass to Pinkston for a touchdown and a 17-6 lead in the third quarter. Then the Eagles added a field goal to win by 14 points.

In the second-to-last game of the season, McNabb led the Eagles to a 24-21 defeat of the New York Giants, with Philadelphia scoring 10 points with less than two minutes to play. With the win, the Eagles clinched the NFC East title. In the final march downfield, McNabb started at the Eagles' 29-yard line with only a minute left in the game. With passes to Thrash and Pinkston and a run on his own, McNabb brought the Eagles to the Giants' 17-yard line. Kicker David Akers then made a field goal to win the game. "He was extremely confident," tight end Chad Lewis told Steve Popper of *The New York Times*, referring to McNabb's performance in the huddle as the Eagles drove downfield in their come-from-behind victory. "He looked everyone in the eyes, and there was no hesitation. He was the leader, fearless. I think everyone on our team drew energy from his eyes in the huddle."

TO THE PLAYOFFS AGAIN

"We're NFC East champs," McNabb told Popper after the game. "It sounds good to us. ... We kept confidence all through the year no matter what happened. We stuck together and kept fighting. That shows right there our heart and determination."

In a rematch of the previous season, the Eagles met Tampa Bay in the wild-card game at Veterans Stadium in Philadelphia—with the same result, a victory over the Buccaneers. As *New York Times* reporter Jeré Longman wrote, "Boos [when McNabb was drafted] have long since turned to reverential cheers. Thousands of fans wear McNabb's No. 5 jersey to Veterans Stadium, and they chant 'MVP, MVP' when he steps onto the field." McNabb outwitted the Buccaneers with a 39-yard run during the first quarter and footwork that enabled him to sidestep would-be Tampa Bay tacklers throughout the game. Although the Buccaneer defenders chased McNabb out of the pocket, he still completed a touchdown pass to tight end Chad Lewis—one of two he completed on the way to a 31-9 trouncing of Tampa Bay.

The next playoff game brought the Eagles to Soldier Field in Chicago for a game against the Bears. Chicago was home for McNabb; his parents lived there. And his mother, Wilma, prepared a home-cooked meal for his teammates in their hotel room. According to Dave Anderson of *The New York Times*, the meal included red beans and rice with sausages. "They've also ordered fried chicken, turkey, macaroni and cheese, peach cobbler," McNabb said, "and cornbread with extra butter. My mom's bringing everything." Perhaps it was the home-cooked meal that helped the Eagles defeat the Bears, 33-19.

Playing in front of a hometown crowd, McNabb threw for 262 yards and two touchdowns. He also rushed the ball 37 yards on eight carries. As one of the Bears' defensive players put it after the game, "He beat us. He beat us running. He beat us throwing," according to *Philadelphia Inquirer* reporter Frank Fitzpatrick. "A couple of times, I did see where he was running and ended up throwing the ball to a guy who was wide open. I don't know what happened, but he was very successful."

Dunking the ball over the goalpost, Donovan McNabb celebrated his fourth-quarter touchdown against the Chicago Bears in their playoff game on January 19, 2002. With their 33-19 win, the Eagles moved on to the NFC Championship Game.

The Eagles had only one more hurdle—the NFC Championship Game against the St. Louis Rams—and they could head to the Super Bowl. Philadelphia held the lead at halftime 17-13, after McNabb completed a scoring pass to Todd Pinkston. But the Rams came roaring back, winning the game in the second half. The final score was 29-24. Once again, for the Eagles and Donovan McNabb, it was wait until next year.

Personal and Professional Life

In May 2002, during the off-season, Donovan McNabb became engaged to Raquel-Ann Sarah Nurse, nicknamed Roxi. The couple had met while attending Syracuse University. "She was just the little scrawny one in class," McNabb said, according to Jenice Armstrong of the *Philadelphia Daily News.* At 5 feet, 5 inches (165 centimeters), Nurse played point guard for the Syracuse women's basketball team. She became one of the greatest women's players in Syracuse history, with a record 530 assists. She was also a leading academic scholar, a member of the Big East Academic All-Star team for three years, and in 1997–1998, the Big East scholar athlete of the year.

As teammate Teakyta Barnes told Armstrong, "She came into Syracuse with her mind set, 'I'm going to take advantage of everything that's given to me.'" Born in Hamilton, Ontario, Canada, Nurse was one of eight children—the youngest child of Arlie and Marjorie Nurse. She learned how to play basketball by competing against her older brothers. "My brothers were the ones who gave me my first basketball and made me tough," she told Armstrong.

At Syracuse, McNabb and Nurse "were always together," according to Barnes. "They would go to each other's games when they weren't playing. They would always go to eat together, go to the movies. … They were in love, but it wasn't a high-profile relationship. They didn't want everyone on campus to know. She's a quiet person. She doesn't like to be in the limelight." They also went jogging together, studied together, and played basketball. "He liked to win, and she liked to win," Barnes added. "They are two competitive people."

After graduation, Nurse went to work at Villanova University in the Philadelphia suburbs. She was responsible for providing counseling and academic assistance for approximately 600 athletes at Villanova. Eventually, she hoped to become an athletic director at a university.

McNabb proposed to Roxi when the couple was on a cruise in the Caribbean Sea. "We're overjoyed about Roxi," Wilma McNabb told columnist Stu Bykofsky of the *Philadelphia Daily News*, "because we've known her for a while, we know her family, we know her, and Roxi was around before Donovan was 'Mr. Donovan, NFL Quarterback.'" Roxi and Donovan were married about a year later in June 2003, in Oak Forest, Illinois, outside Chicago, and McNabb's brother was the best man. The wedding was attended by McNabb's teammates on the Philadelphia Eagles as well as coach Andy Reid and his wife, Frank Lenti from Mt. Carmel High School, Paul Pasqualoni from Syracuse University, and Eagles owner Jeffrey Lurie. The wedding was followed by a lavish reception for 300 guests at the Ritz-Carlton in Chicago.

2002–2003 SEASON

The exciting events in McNabb's personal life did not prevent him from staying focused on a new football season. Soon after his engagement, McNabb signed a new contract with the Eagles for 12 years and $115 million. And with McNabb at the helm, the Eagles hoped that this year might end with a trip to the Super Bowl. But 2002 started poorly, with the Eagles losing 27-24 to the Tennessee Titans. McNabb was sacked six times and threw two interceptions. Nevertheless, he also completed three touchdown passes.

The next three games, however, were different, as McNabb led the team to victories over the Washington Redskins, the Dallas Cowboys, and the Houston Texans. In the Washington game, McNabb had four completions in the Eagles' first touchdown drive, including a 33-yard pass to James Thrash. Then he faked a pass and ran the ball into the end zone. "I felt comfortable and relaxed out there," he told Thomas George of *The New York Times*. "Our receivers were getting [open], and the line was giving me time to run and pass. This is something to build on." He followed this with three touchdowns passes against Dallas in a 44-13 blowout. On another play, McNabb faked to a fullback, then made an option pitch to running back Brian Westbrook, who threw a 25-yard touchdown pass to Todd Pinkston.

McNabb threw for a total of six touchdowns and more than 800 yards in the three games. The Eagles also relied on the rushing of Westbrook and Duce Staley. After losing to the Jacksonville Jaguars, 28-25, and defeating the Tampa Bay Buccaneers, the Eagles found themselves atop the NFC East with a 4–2 record.

One of the team's most impressive victories came against the New York Giants late in October. In that game, McNabb rushed for more than 100 yards, capped by a 40-yard run for a touchdown, as the Eagles won 17-3. Philadelphia followed that victory with another hard-fought win against the Chicago

Eagles center Hank Fraley reached down to Donovan McNabb after he was injured on the third play of a game on November 17, 2002, against the Arizona Cardinals. McNabb broke his ankle on the play, but he remained in the game and threw four touchdown passes in leading the Eagles to a 38-14 win.

Bears, 19-13. The Eagles were riding high until a home game against Arizona in November. There, in a victory over the Cardinals, McNabb was hurt on the third play of the game. Nevertheless he went back onto the field and guided the team to a 38-14 victory.

McNabb downplayed the injury, and at first he did not think it was very serious. As Selena Roberts of *The New York Times* put it, he is a "quarterback with the pain threshold of a Hummer," and he "pronounced himself fit to roll." Although he was limping and could not rely on his classic scrambles, McNabb was deadly from the pocket, and during the game, he completed four touchdown passes. But X-rays later showed that he had broken his ankle, and it looked as if McNabb would be forced out of action for the rest of the season. The Eagles would have to rely on backup quarterbacks Koy Detmer and A.J. Feeley.

As reporter Thomas George of *The New York Times* explained, injuries to starting quarterbacks highlight the importance of having backups who can step into the role. During the first 12 weeks of the season, George added, many teams were forced to make substitutions at the quarterback position. "Some of the changes have been made because of performance, and many more are the result of injury."

In the next game, against the San Francisco 49ers, Detmer passed for two touchdowns and rushed for another score in helping to lead the Eagles to a 38-17 win. But Detmer dislocated his left elbow late in the game, and Feeley, the third-string quarterback, would now be taking snaps.

In his first game, against St. Louis in early December, Feeley passed for only 181 yards, in a 10-3 Eagles victory, largely due to the strength of the Philadelphia defense. But Philadelphia kept winning behind Feeley, and completed the season with three more victories before a season-ending 10-7 loss to the Giants.

ONE MORE TRY IN THE PLAYOFFS

Finishing the season at 12–4, the Eagles prepared to face the Atlanta Falcons in the playoffs. By this time McNabb had begun to work out again—45 days after his ankle had been broken in Arizona. His quick recovery was helped by a vigorous workout routine. According to Michael Silver of *Sports Illustrated*, his "workouts at the team facility were so intense that tired trainers had to administer his exercises in shifts."

Atlanta traveled to Veterans Stadium in Philadelphia, where they faced the Eagles on a frigid 20°F (-7°C) day. In the first series of plays from scrimmage deep in Philadelphia territory, McNabb was forced back into the end zone. Trying to

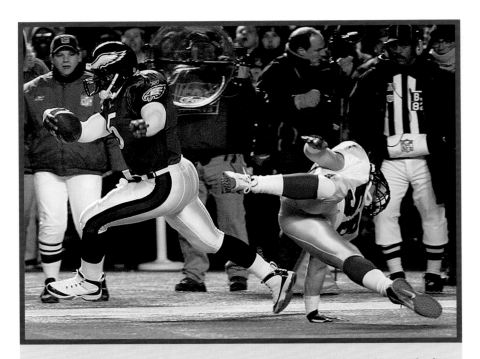

Donovan McNabb scrambled past Atlanta Falcons linebacker Keith Brooking in the first quarter of an NFC playoff game on January 11, 2003. The game was McNabb's first since he broke his ankle nearly two months before. Once his teammates saw him running, they knew that McNabb was back.

escape from Falcon strong safety Gerald McBurrows, McNabb finally slipped across the end line and ran up the **sidelines** for 19 yards. "Move, baby, move!" yelled Wilma McNabb from her seat in the stands, according to Michael Silver. His father was also excited, "That's what I'm talkin' about!" he said after the play. "That run was what I was waiting to see," added Eagles wideout Antonio Freeman. "When I saw that, I said, 'He's back,' and I'm sure everyone else did, too."

But it was not McNabb's rushing that made the difference in the game. It was his passing—247 yards with no interceptions and one touchdown—that helped Philadelphia win the game 20-6.

After the victory over Atlanta, Philadelphia faced Tampa Bay in the NFC title game. They had beaten the Buccaneers in past years during the playoffs. And the Eagles hoped to win one more contest on their way to the Super Bowl. But Philadelphia lost this one 27-10. After the game, McNabb was criticized by fans who thought that his 45-day layoff had not given him enough time to prepare. They also wondered if his ankle had not recovered fully enough for him to scramble away from the powerful, defensive front four of Tampa Bay.

"I'm pretty sure he took it [the loss] hard," Eagles safety Brian Dawkins told *USA Today*. Added cornerback Troy Vincent, "The quarterback gets the glory when we win, and he gets the blame when we lose. You can't put the game on his back. Collectively, we didn't get it done." McNabb tried to stay upbeat and began to look ahead to the next season. "Hopefully, the third time's a charm," he said after the Eagles dropped their second NFC title game in a row. "That's what we have to think in the off-season. We know how to get there. Now let's take that extra step. Obviously, we'll put it behind us and start all over."

THE 2003 SEASON

But as the 2003 season began, McNabb and the Eagles did not start "all over" the way that they had hoped. Philadelphia was playing in a new stadium, Lincoln Financial Field, just across the street from Veterans Stadium. The new stadium had cost more than $520 million to build. In the first game, though, the Eagles were crushed by their old nemesis—Tampa Bay. McNabb could only manage 148 passing yards in a 17-0 defeat, and he kept throwing **incomplete passes** to his receivers.

The second game was no better. As *New York Times* reporter Damon Hack wrote, "Donovan McNabb kept looking at his throwing hand, looking for answers it refused to provide. He rubbed his palm. He licked his fingers. … In the third quarter, when the impatient crowd had finally had its fill, the fans began to chant 'A.J! A.J!' a reference to A.J. Feeley, the third quarterback on the Philadelphia Eagles … who posted a 4–1 record when McNabb was injured last season."

As McNabb himself admitted to Hack, "These last two weeks are nowhere near how I've been playing the last two years. I'm surprised by it. What's happened these last two weeks is just not me." As coach Andy Reid explained to the press after a 31-10 loss to the New England Patriots, "It's not just Donovan. Please don't point the finger at him. It goes around to everybody." Finally, the Eagles bounced back in their third game, beating the Buffalo Bills 23-13. The damage, though,

McNABB VS. LIMBAUGH

For the 2003 season, ESPN hired conservative radio personality Rush Limbaugh as a commentator on its program *Sunday NFL Countdown*. After the first two Eagle losses of the season, Limbaugh was highly critical of McNabb. "I don't think he's been that good from the get-go," Limbaugh said, according to James Alder of the Web site About.Com: Football. "I think what we've had here is a little social concern in the NFL. The media has been very desirous that a black quarterback do well. They're interested in black coaches and black quarterbacks doing well. … McNabb got a lot of the credit for the performance of the team that he really didn't deserve."

As Alder explained, "This is what ESPN hired him [Limbaugh] to do. Create controversy for the sake of ratings. Never mind the fact that he doesn't know what he's talking about, as long as it results in a few extra dollars in the network's coffers they'll allow him to continue making … statements that have no factual basis." Since joining the team in 1999, McNabb had not only helped improve its record every had been done; Philadelphia fans and the sports media were expressing serious doubts about McNabb's ability to run the Eagles' offense.

Over the next several weeks, critical comments made by Rush Limbaugh against McNabb seemed to light a spark in the Eagles' season. They ran off a string of victories, capped by a 17-14 come-from-behind triumph over the Green Bay Packers in mid-November. With less than three minutes remaining, Philadelphia took over the football on its own 35-yard line. McNabb completed passes to Duce Staley and Chad Lewis,

year, he had also led the Eagles to two NFC Championship Games. He had thrown more than 70 touchdown passes and scored 14 touchdowns rushing.

At first, ESPN said nothing. But Limbaugh's comments were heavily criticized in the press. Finally ESPN said that his comments had been "insensitive and inappropriate." Shortly afterward, Limbaugh resigned from the network.

Meanwhile, McNabb handled the entire incident very calmly. During a news conference, he said, "I don't think he was the only one that felt that way, and I'm sure there are a lot of people that feel the same way and are afraid to say it," according to Clifton Brown of *The New York Times*. "It's sad that you've got to go to skin color," he added. "I thought we were through with that whole deal."

Eagles tight end Chad Lewis praised McNabb. "Donovan stood up and handled that situation with class. ... Rush came after him. He didn't come after anyone else. He came after Donovan, and Donovan handled it."

completing the drive with a six-yard pass to Todd Pinkston with less than 30 seconds remaining in the game.

By the end of the month, Philadelphia had climbed to 8–3 and had moved into a four-way tie for the best record in the National Football Conference. "I always said things would turn out positive," McNabb told Dave Caldwell of *The New York Times*. In Week 12, the Eagles defeated the Carolina Panthers, 25-16, for their seventh victory in a row. McNabb threw for 182 yards, including a touchdown pass to James Thrash in the fourth quarter. "There's no time to go wild," McNabb cautioned his team after the victory, according to reporter Viv Bernstein of *The New York Times*. "You go wild in February [after the Super Bowl]. It's all about winning and moving on."

Looking back at the season, Matt Crossman of *Sporting News* praised McNabb for staying focused and not giving up even in the face of severe criticism. "Donovan McNabb turned his season around not with a dramatic play or a big game but with perseverance," Crossman wrote. "He showed up for practice every day and worked and worked. The improvement came slowly, sporadically, in fits and starts." After a slow beginning, McNabb started to pass for more than 300 yards in games. "Never has it been more obvious how important McNabb is to the Eagles," Crossman added. "He sets the tone on offense, and the better he has gotten, the better his teammates have gotten."

In December, McNabb led the Eagles to a 36-10 victory over the Dallas Cowboys, their eighth victory in a row. They scored 26 points in the second half, as McNabb threw for three touchdowns in the game. One went to Duce Staley, who made a valiant second effort after being hit by a defender to cross the goal line. The win against Dallas was followed by two convincing victories against Miami and Washington.

The Miami win came in a *Monday Night Football* game on ABC. It was a close game, with the Dolphins tying the score

In a December 2003 game, Donovan McNabb ran for a 21-yard gain against the Dallas Cowboys. The Eagles' 36-10 victory was their eighth in a row after a 2–3 start.

at 24-24 in the third quarter. Then McNabb led the Eagles on a 62-yard scoring drive, and Philadelphia placekicker David Akers added a field goal to win the game. As Miami coach Dave Wannstedt told Charlie Nobles of *The New York Times*, McNabb "did a great job avoiding the rush. We had him in our grasp a number of times and he got away."

FIRST PLACE IN THE NFC EAST

With a victory against Washington at the end of the regular season, Philadelphia clinched first place in the NFC East. McNabb threw touchdown passes to tight end Chad Lewis, wide receiver Freddie Mitchell, and running back Correll Buckhalter, while rushing for a touchdown himself in the 31-7 victory. Completing the season at 12–4, Philadelphia seemed to have an excellent shot at earning its first trip to the Super Bowl in many seasons.

But they had to defeat the Green Bay Packers and quarterback Brett Favre in the first playoff game. With just over two minutes left in the game, the Packers held a 17-14 lead. On **fourth down** with only a yard to go, the Packers punted the ball. McNabb then engineered a drive down field that ended with a 37-yard field goal by Akers. That sent the game into **sudden death** overtime, during which Akers kicked another field goal, sealing the victory for Philadelphia.

That victory moved the Eagles one step closer to the Super Bowl. Asked at a news conference after the game whether he was thinking about the championship game, McNabb said, "All the time," according to Dave Caldwell of *The New York Times*. But the Eagles first had to beat the Carolina Panthers in the NFC Championship Game. They had lost two title games in the previous two seasons. "You use that as a little fuel to the fire and go out and know what you have to do to take advantage of the things that are given to you," McNabb told the press. "You make sure you're confident, and the guys see your confidence, and you all rally around each other."

In the game against Carolina, though, McNabb suffered a serious injury to his ribs after being hit by a Panther defender. Although he continued to play, McNabb threw three interceptions, and the Philadelphia offense sputtered. The Eagles could only score a field goal in a 14-3 loss. "It was rough," McNabb said, according to Dave Caldwell of *The New York Times*. "I continued to stay with it and fight through it." But he added: "For me, being a competitor, it [the loss] was tough to swallow."

On to the
Super Bowl

After three disappointing losses in three successive NFC Championship Games, the Eagles decided to strengthen their offense in the off-season. They acquired wide receiver Terrell Owens from the San Francisco 49ers. Born in Alabama in 1973, Owens had played college football at the University of Tennessee at Chattanooga. He joined San Francisco in 1996, rolling up an impressive number of touchdown receptions. But he was also very controversial. Owens had mocked opposing teams on the football field and feuded with 49ers coach Steve Mariucci. In 2004, Owens finally decided to leave San Francisco, and he was picked up by the Eagles.

In the first game of the season, against the New York Giants, Owens got caught in a traffic jam on his way to Lincoln Financial Field and needed a police escort to make it to the

Wide receiver Terrell Owens *(left)* and Donovan McNabb watched the big screen during the fourth quarter of a September 12, 2004, game against the New York Giants. McNabb and Owens connected for three touchdowns in the game. The Eagles had brought in Owens before the season began to give McNabb some offensive weapons.

game. But he played a key role in the 31-17 Eagles victory. Owens caught three touchdown passes—a 20-yarder in the corner of the end zone; a 3-yarder after running across the end zone away from a defender; and a 12-yarder. After each score, Owens put on a performance in the end zone, flapping his arms like an eagle after his third touchdown. The following week, the Eagles went to 2–0 with a victory over the Minnesota Vikings. "What a difference a year makes," McNabb told Judy Battista of *The New York Times*, referring to the previous season when the Eagles lost their first two games. "You could see the confidence out here when we're having a good time." Touchdown passes to Owens and tight end L.J. Smith sealed a 27-16 victory over Minnesota in a *Monday Night Football* game.

Philadelphia continued to win, rolling to a 7–0 record—the first time in Eagles history that they had reached that mark. During that streak, after a 30-13 win over Detroit, McNabb told Damon Hack of *The New York Times,* "Our main goal is to be the No. 1 offense in the league." In that game, he completed 29 passes for 356 yards. Running back Brian Westbrook and Owens continued to be McNabb's favorite receivers. In a close game against the Cleveland Browns, McNabb completed a 28-yard scramble in overtime that set up a winning field goal by David Akers. "I prefer not to run," McNabb told *The New York Times,* "but I have to take full advantage of every opportunity." The Eagles' seven-game winning streak came to an end with a 27-3 loss to the Pittsburgh Steelers. Still, the Eagles had gotten off to an impressive start.

Nevertheless, the victories were accompanied by controversy surrounding Owens. In a skit that opened a *Monday Night Football* game in November, Owens appeared in his locker room with Nicollette Sheridan, a star of the ABC program *Desperate Housewives.* Sheridan, who was wearing only a towel, was trying to tempt Owens to remain with her rather than play in an upcoming game. Owens was criticized for appearing in the skit. As Indianapolis Colts coach Tony Dungy told The Associated Press, "If that's what we have to do to get [high television] ratings, I'd rather not get them." But, when asked about the commercial, McNabb refused to criticize his teammate.

Later in November, Philadelphia hosted the Washington Redskins at Lincoln Financial Field. After a slow start, McNabb threw four touchdown passes in a 28-6 victory. "It took some time, but we were able to get it done," he told David Picker of *The New York Times*. McNabb was sacked three times by the Redskins, who drove him out of the pocket over and over again, forcing him to scramble. "He took some shots and didn't flinch," said the Eagles' Chad Lewis. "He kept on swinging." McNabb completed two touchdowns to Brian Westbrook in the fourth quarter and hit receiver Todd Pinkston five times for 106 yards.

The Eagles followed this victory by trouncing the New York Giants 27-6 at Giants Stadium. Although McNabb had a fumble, he completed a touchdown pass and ran for another score. The victory gave the Eagles the division title in the NFC East, five weeks before the end of the season. "This says a lot for our team and organization that we continue to fight," McNabb told Bill Finley of *The New York Times*, "after what's happened three straight years," when the Eagles lost in the NFC Championship Game. "We're excited about winning this game, we're excited about clinching, and we're excited about the opportunity to try to get better. There are a lot of things for us to work on. There is consistency on the offensive side, in the running and passing games."

The Eagles did not let down after clinching the division. In early December, they overwhelmed the Green Bay Packers 47-17. McNabb led the Eagles to a 35-0 halftime lead, completing his first 14 passes. As Al Harris, the Packers cornerback, told Jeré Longman of *The New York Times*, "Guys had him [McNabb] in the grasp, he still made plays. Every time he saw a soft spot in our zone, he hit it. He made a lot of great reads." Many of these reads resulted in completed passes to Owens and Westbrook. Owens scored his fourteenth touchdown of the season and completed his seventh game with 100 yards in receptions.

Later in December, Owens was hurt after catching a pass in the third quarter of a game against the Dallas Cowboys. He was pulled down from behind by a Dallas defender, holding his right knee as he fell. Owens had suffered a sprained ankle and a fractured fibula in his right leg, which put him out for the rest of the season. Philadelphia lost two games later in the month, finishing the season at 13–3.

THE PLAYOFFS

Before the playoffs began, McNabb went to Arizona, where he and his wife have a home. He wanted to rest in the warm, sunny December weather. As Paul Attner of *Sporting News* wrote, "He now is a quarterback with the sufficient experience, technique, and will to control the conference playoffs."

In the divisional playoff game, the Eagles faced the Minnesota Vikings. Early in the game, McNabb completed a two-yard touchdown pass to Freddie Mitchell for a 7-0 lead. After another scoring drive, McNabb led the Eagles into Minnesota territory again and threw a pass to tight end L.J. Smith near the 10-yard line. When Smith was hit, the ball shot into the air but it was recovered by Mitchell in the end zone, giving Philadelphia a 21-7 lead. "I've always felt Freddie [Mitchell] was doing an excellent job," McNabb told Longman of *The New York Times*. "It just so happens he gets overshadowed. He's stepped into the role of starting receiver [after Owens was injured] and made big things happen." Meanwhile, the Eagle defense repeatedly used the blitz to stop Viking quarterback Daunte Culpepper and sack him. One of these sacks, by safety Brian Dawkins, pushed the Vikings back out of field-goal range. As Eagles cornerback Sheldon Brown told Josh Elliot of *Sports Illustrated*, "There's someone inside Dawk that we only see on Sundays. We feed off that. He's our leader [on defense]. Period." It was too much for the Vikings, and Philadelphia won the game 27-14.

McNabb and the Eagles then prepared themselves for the NFC Championship Game, which they had lost three years in a row. This time they faced the Atlanta Falcons, led by quarterback Michael Vick. It was the first time that two African-American quarterbacks—McNabb and Vick—had met each other in a NFC Championship Game.

On the night before the game, coach Andy Reid told his team, "Enjoy the moment. Enjoy playing together. Do what

WILMA AND SAM—A DYNAMIC DUO

Wilma and Sam McNabb are not content to simply attend Eagles football games and watch their son play—although Wilma admits that she still worries before every game. "We pray as a family before every game," she wrote in *Sporting News*. "If it's a home game, we meet at Donovan's house and put him in the middle. Then we make a circle—me, my husband, Donovan's wife, any friends who have traveled in for the game—and say a prayer that Donovan stays safe. If it's an away game, we do it at the team hotel." At the games, Wilma also wears a jersey with Donovan's number on it—5. "When Donovan gets hit," she added, "I know the player who did it. I know his number, his name, everything."

Eagles football, however, is only part of Wilma's life. In 2000, Donovan started the Donovan McNabb Foundation to raise awareness about diabetes. Wilma McNabb's mother died of diabetes, and Sam McNabb was diagnosed with the disease in the 1990s. Wilma McNabb runs the foundation, which works closely with the American Diabetes Association. It provides large donations to the association's camp program for children with diabetes. Wilma McNabb also organizes fundraising events and programs to educate people about the dangers of diabetes and the importance of supporting efforts to combat the disease.

you do," according to Peter King of *Sports Illustrated.* The next day was very cold with the wind chill bringing the temperature down to -5°F (-20°C) in Philadelphia.

McNabb had an exceptional game, converting seven of 14 third downs into **first downs**. He tossed two touchdowns to tight end Chad Lewis. But Lewis hurt his right leg while

"Diabetes is a serious disease, and it can be especially tough on kids," said McNabb, according to the American Diabetes Association. "But with positive education programs and activities like those provided at American Diabetes Association camps, kids with diabetes can learn to be more comfortable about who they are and what they need to do to manage their disease."

Sam and Wilma also keep busy in other ways. He is a co-founder and president of the National Football Players Fathers Association, while she is vice president of the Professional Football Players Mothers Association. The purpose of both organizations is to get parents more involved in the careers of their sons. For those players without involved parents, the associations solicit help from other men and women to act as role models. As Sam told D.A. Sears, managing editor of *In Search of Fatherhood,* "As a father of an existing player, I have noticed how unstable and self-centered some of the young men without prominent male figures in their lives are, and I have also noticed that they make poor decisions both on and off the field." The association works with the NFL to provide "guidance for both our sons and any other professional football players who desired to have a positive male figure in their lives."

Donovan McNabb and Jeffrey Lurie, the owner of the Eagles, celebrated in January 2005 after Philadelphia won the NFC Championship Game 27-10 over the Atlanta Falcons. After three straight losses in the NFC title game, the Eagles would now play in the Super Bowl.

making his second touchdown catch and was out for the rest of the season. Meanwhile, the Eagles' defense contained the Falcons for much of the game, preventing Vick from reaching the outside so he could not run. As they went to the locker room after the game, a 27-10 Philadelphia victory, the Eagles yelled, "'One more! One more!" according to King. The Eagles and McNabb had finally reached the goal that had eluded them so often in the past—the Super Bowl.

THE SUPER BOWL

In getting them there, McNabb completed an incredible season, passing for 31 touchdowns and running for three scores. He was the only quarterback in the history of the National Football League to throw at least 30 touchdown receptions while having fewer than 10 interceptions (he had eight for the season). Part of his success was due to Terrell Owens, who caught 14 touchdown passes before he was injured. Although he missed the two playoff games, Owens returned for the Super Bowl game against the New England Patriots.

As the Eagles went to the Super Bowl, McNabb was only one of three African-American quarterbacks to lead his team into the championship. As McNabb put it, "I feel great to be a part of that," according to *USA Today* reporter Jarrett Bell. "I think it's a special feeling, not only for myself, but for all of the African-American quarterbacks that are in the NFL, as well as playing on the collegiate level. I think it gives an extra push of motivation. It gives (African-American) quarterbacks a drive on the collegiate level to know that this can happen to them."

A SUPER BOWL LOSS AND A CONTROVERSY

But even that drive was not enough to give McNabb and the Eagles the edge that they needed. In a close game, they lost 24-21 to the New England Patriots. McNabb took a lot of the blame for the loss as the Eagles offense did not seem to play with much urgency in trying to come back in the fourth quarter. In Philadelphia, the media called it the "worst big-game performance ... ever seen," according to Henry Marcus, a reporter with the *New York Amsterdam News.* As Marcus put it, "The road to respectability has been a rough one for Donovan McNabb. ... For the black quarterback, winning the Super Bowl is probably the only way to have a shot at being named with the greats, and even that may not do it."

Shortly after the Eagles' loss in the Super Bowl, Terrell Owens also criticized McNabb for his performance. "I'm not the one who got tired at the Super Bowl," Owens said, according to Clifton Brown of *The New York Times.* Owens was referring to the fact that McNabb seemed to have lost some of his energy near the end of the fourth quarter and might have even been sick. Meanwhile, Owens had also told the Eagles that he was unhappy with the $49 million contract he had signed a year earlier. Owens' agent, Drew Rosenhaus, planned to meet with Eagles president Joe Banner and coach Andy Reid to try to renegotiate a better deal for Owens. But they refused to change the terms of the original agreement.

At the Eagles' summer camp in August, McNabb and Owens went through the practice drills together, but they were barely speaking to each other. Nevertheless, McNabb told reporters that he had no intention of letting their conflict over his Super Bowl performance get in the way of the 2005 season. According to Clifton Brown, he said, "When T.O. [Terrell Owens] is on the football field, T.O. is focused on what he has to do. I can't speak on behalf of when he is off the field. But when he is on the football field, he is going to work."

McNabb himself had put in a tough off-season workout session in Arizona before coming to training camp. He led the program, which included other professional athletes as well as college and high school players. "Donovan makes it so much fun," said NBA star forward Richard Jefferson. "It almost doesn't seem like work," he added, according to reporters Jeffri Chadiha and Bill Syken of *Sports Illustrated.*

One season later, and the relationship between Donovan McNabb and Terrell Owens had chilled considerably. Here, Owens walks past McNabb during training camp in August 2005. Owens had criticized McNabb's performance in the Super Bowl and was unhappy with his contract with the Eagles.

Once the preseason games began, McNabb demonstrated that all of his preparation had been worthwhile. In a game against the Cincinnati Bengals, he threw a 64-yard touchdown pass to Owens in a 27-17 victory. McNabb also completed two more touchdown passes and threw for 256 yards in the game. Nevertheless, as the regular season began, the Eagles faced a variety of problems. Owens had caused conflicts in training camp, where he was ordered to leave temporarily after an argument with Reid. And Todd Pinkston, one of the Eagles' receivers, suffered an injury to his **Achilles tendon** that put him out for the rest of the season.

THE REGULAR SEASON BEGINS

McNabb still had Owens in the lineup, even if the two men did not get along. He also had Brian Westbrook, the Eagles' star running back, as well as a trio of young receivers—Greg Lewis, Billy McMullen, and Reggie Brown. It was not enough, however, to get the Eagles off to an impressive start. In the first game, Owens caught seven passes for 112 yards, and Westbrook caught a McNabb pass for a touchdown. But the Eagles still lost to Atlanta 14-10.

Over the next several weeks, however, Philadelphia bounced back, reeling off a string of victories. In a game against the Kansas City Chiefs, the Eagles came from 18 points down— they were trailing 24-6 in the second quarter—to win 37-31. McNabb threw for 369 yards and three touchdowns, giving his team a record of 3–1 in the early part of the season. It looked as if Philadelphia might be on its way to another Super Bowl.

PLAYING HURT

Then the season began to fall apart. In an overwhelming loss to Dallas, 33-10, McNabb was sacked four times and only managed to throw for 131 yards. McNabb was playing with a serious injury, which may have contributed to his performance on the field. He had a sports hernia, a tear in a muscle in his abdomen. Dr. William Meyers, chief of surgery at Drexel University in Philadelphia, was treating McNabb for the injury. "You get pain from the injury itself and pain in other locations as the body tries to compensate," Meyers told

Michael Bradley of *Sporting News*. The hernia made bending very difficult for McNabb.

McNabb refused to stop playing or undergo surgery, which would have put him out of action for 8 to 12 weeks. "If I can't lead us to where we want to go," he told Tom Pedulla of *USA Today*, "I feel I'm not complete. It's sad we're measured by the number of championships we won, but that is the ultimate prize." According to Pedulla, McNabb also decided not to take any painkillers. He said it was better to "get used to pain instead of finding something that is going to cover it up for a couple of hours and then when it wears off, it feels like you've really been stabbed." Added to the hernia, McNabb also had bruised his chest and shin.

In addition to McNabb's physical problems, the situation with Owens was getting worse. In an interview with ESPN, Owens said that Brett Favre, quarterback of the Green Bay Packers, could be doing a better job with the Eagles than McNabb had done so far in the season. McNabb later told Michael Smith of ESPN.com, "It was definitely a slap in the face to me. … And to say if we had Brett Favre, that could mean that if you had another quarterback of a different descent or ethnic background, we could be winning."

Meanwhile, Owens had also been in a fight with one of his teammates in the locker room and criticized the Eagles for not showing him more appreciation for his performance on the field. In Week 9, Philadelphia finally suspended Owens from play for four games. Later he apologized, saying, "I would like to reiterate my respect for Donovan McNabb, as a quarterback, and as a teammate," according to Clifton Brown of *The New York Times*. "I would like to apologize to him for any comments that may have been negative." But the suspension remained in effect.

Eventually, Coach Reid decided that the Eagles would not allow Owens to come back to the team. As Eagles safety Brian Dawkins told Clifton Brown afterward, "Call me naïve, but I

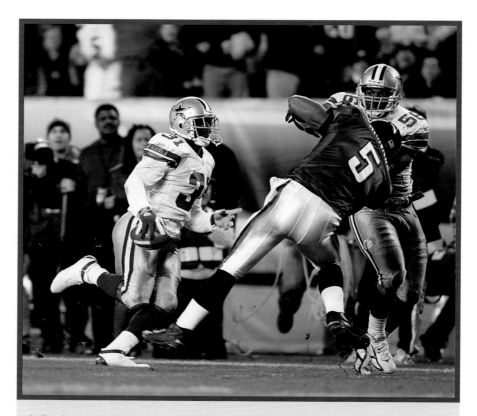

Dallas linebacker Bradie James blocked Donovan McNabb as safety Roy Williams *(left)* returned an interception late in the fourth quarter of a game on November 14, 2005. McNabb had been suffering from a sports hernia all season. He aggravated his injury on this play. Soon after, McNabb decided to have surgery, forcing him to miss the rest of the season.

was really believing that he was going to come here, and we were going to win a Super Bowl, and we were going to continue to roll, and there would be no issues—period. He was going to understand what we have here as a team and what we are as a unit and tight bunch. I thought he would understand that, and there would not be any problems." It was a tough decision for the Eagles to remove Owens. He had been a top performer on the field and helped Philadelphia reach the Super Bowl in the previous season. But Reid had put the unity of his team ahead of the importance of one player—no matter how talented he was.

A SEASON WITHOUT OWENS AND McNABB

But without Owens, the Eagles lost a close game 21-20 to the Dallas Cowboys on *Monday Night Football*. With less than three minutes left in the game, McNabb threw a pass that was intercepted by Roy Williams, who took the ball in for the winning touchdown. With McNabb managing to throw for only 169 yards in the game against the Cowboys, Philadelphia fell to 4–5 on the season. After throwing the interception, McNabb aggravated his sports hernia. And he finally decided to put an end to his season. Late in November, the Eagles told the media that McNabb had scheduled surgery on the hernia. "I'm disappointed that the injury has reached this stage and has ultimately ended my season," McNabb said, according to Clifton Brown. "I wanted so much to help this team turn it around and was unable to do that."

Without a healthy McNabb, the Eagles failed to turn their season around, completing 2005 with a losing 6–10 record. In December, Philadelphia was shut out by the Seattle Seahawks 42-0—an embarrassing loss and the worst in Coach Reid's career with Philadelphia. The entire season was a big comedown for a team that had gone to the Super Bowl only a year earlier. Meanwhile, McNabb underwent extensive surgery by Dr. Meyers, who later pronounced the operation a complete success. All McNabb could do at this point was to look forward to a better season in 2006.

A Great
Pro Quarterback
and His Future

After the conflicts with Terrell Owens and a season-ending injury, Donovan McNabb needed time to relax, recover, and reflect. In February 2006, while he was recovering from surgery, McNabb sat down for a long interview with Michael Smith of ESPN. He was asked a series of questions about the Owens incident, how he—McNabb—had handled it, and its impact on the Philadelphia Eagles.

"It led to the team being separated. It led to a lot of things happening that were uncharacteristic of everybody. I tried to handle it in a fashion to where everyone understood that you can't let some things bother you. But when it bothers others, it can lead to what happened to us this year." McNabb believed that the events surrounding Owens had divided the Eagles. Players lined up and took sides—supporting Owens or supporting McNabb. The teamwork necessary to produce a winning football team became impossible to achieve.

McNabb believed that the problem with Owens had begun as early as the twelfth week of the previous season, in 2004, when Philadelphia beat the Giants. McNabb said that he had "dropped back five steps, looked downfield, at that time I didn't feel he [Owens] came open, and checked [threw] it down to [Brian] Westbrook. It was an incomplete pass." Owens returned to the huddle, complaining that he had been open and McNabb should have passed him the ball. Although McNabb told him to get into the huddle so he could call the next play, Owens kept complaining.

"That's where I feel it all started," McNabb told Smith. "That's where maybe he felt like I was bigger than anything. But I'm a competitor. That's my huddle. I'm trying to lead us in the right direction."

The conflict, McNabb believed, undermined his position as leader of the Philadelphia Eagles. The team broke down into "cliques," McNabb said. Some players began to talk about him behind his back and to support Owens. At the end of the interview, however, McNabb said that he had put the 2005 season behind him and was looking forward to 2006. Since Owens had been released by the Eagles and had signed with Dallas, the situation was improving. "We have to get confidence back to Five [the number on McNabb's jersey]." He said that all the players were rallying around him again—"which is cool. I work with everybody."

In July, Owens published his version of what happened in Philadelphia in a book titled *T.O.* He accused McNabb of being an ineffective quarterback and said that McNabb and coach Andy Reid had caused all of Owens's problems at Philadelphia. "I accept that I played a role in tearing apart the Eagles' season," he told NBC, "but the blame was not all mine."

McNabb seemed to pay little attention to the book. At training camp in August, he was focused on preparing himself

Donovan McNabb and receiver Reggie Brown shared a laugh during the Eagles' training camp in July 2006 in Bethlehem, Pennsylvania. After the Terrell Owens controversy and the dismal 2005 season, McNabb's teammates were glad to see him smiling again.

for a winning season. McNabb's laughter was heard throughout the Eagles locker room—a sure sign, according to linebacker Jeremiah Trotter, that he was ready for the 2006 season. "He seems to have put it all behind him and be the Donovan we all know, laughing, joking, having fun," Trotter told Tom Pedulla of *USA Today*. "When he's like that, he's at his best."

Indeed, McNabb had much to be proud of during his years as the Eagles' quarterback. He had led the team to a 60–28 record—the best among quarterbacks who had appeared in 80 or more games. He had also won more playoff games than any other quarterback who had ever played for the Eagles. Nevertheless, he was still being criticized by reporters in

Philadelphia for not winning the Super Bowl. McNabb hoped to solve that problem in 2006.

THE 2006 SEASON BEGINS

As if to show that he was fully recovered, McNabb led the Eagles to a 24-10 victory in the opening game against the Houston Texans. One of his favorite receivers was Donte' Stallworth, who had replaced Owens. He caught the ball six times, once for a touchdown, as McNabb threw for 314 yards. Philadelphia, though, was not as successful in its next game—a loss to the New York Giants. The Eagles allowed a 24-7 lead in the fourth quarter to slip away, and the Giants won the game in overtime.

The Eagles bounced back, winning their next two games. On *Monday Night Football*, McNabb led them to an impressive 31-9 win over the Green Bay Packers and their quarterback Brett Favre. Behind by 9-7 at the half, McNabb tried to fire up the team in the locker room, Reid told reporter Jim Corbett of *USA Today*. "At halftime, [McNabb] got after the guys a little bit." McNabb told them: "'Hey, pick your heads up; let's go. Kick it into gear,'" Reid said. "That's what good leaders do." The Eagles came out and scored 24 unanswered points, with McNabb throwing for 288 yards and two touchdowns to receiver Greg Lewis, while scoring twice on runs of 6 and 15 yards.

In the next game against the Dallas Cowboys, Philadelphia fans were wondering what might happen when McNabb and Terrell Owens found themselves on opposing teams. Although Owens caught three passes, the day belonged to McNabb. He passed for 354 yards at Lincoln Financial Field, as the Eagles won 38-24. "We feel like we're getting better in our passing game," McNabb told Skip Wood of *USA Today*. He praised the Eagles' Greg Lewis, one of seven receivers who had caught one or more passes in the game. "They're guys that I feel confident in," McNabb added. "They work extremely hard, and they prepare themselves to be the best, and that's all I ask."

After the victory against Dallas, however, the Eagles seemed to slide downhill—losing games to New Orleans, Tampa Bay, and Jacksonville. After the Jaguars beat the Eagles 13-6, Reid called the game "embarrassing," according to *New York Times* reporter Michael Weinreb, as the Eagles fell to 4–4 on the season.

Although the Eagles began to win again, disaster struck in a game against the Tennessee Titans in mid-November. During the game, McNabb suffered an injury to a ligament in his right knee. The injury required extensive knee surgery and meant that McNabb was finished for the rest of the season.

Fortunately, the Eagles had an effective backup quarterback—36-year-old Jeff Garcia—who was ready to step in and replace McNabb. He led Philadelphia to three consecutive victories, improving their record to 8–6. In a game against the Carolina Panthers in early December, Garcia threw three touchdown passes as the Eagles won 27-24. "I really feel something special is taking place right here, right now, for me," Garcia told Tom Pedulla of *USA Today*. "You really see his veteran experience come into play," Reid added. "When you lose a quarterback like Donovan, that is not always the case. But in Jeff, you've got somebody who steps up and grabs everybody and shakes them a little and says, 'Let's go. We're going to be all right.'" Indeed, Garcia's effort in the Carolina game was comparable to McNabb's best performances.

Philadelphia ended the season at 10–6, winning the NFC East title and going to the playoffs. In the wild-card game against the New York Giants, Philadelphia won a close contest, 23-20. Then they suffered a loss to the New Orleans Saints, 27-24. Once again, the Eagles had come up just short of a championship.

2007 FOOTBALL SEASON

As the Eagles advanced to the playoffs and McNabb was recovering from his injury, Wilma McNabb was worrying about her

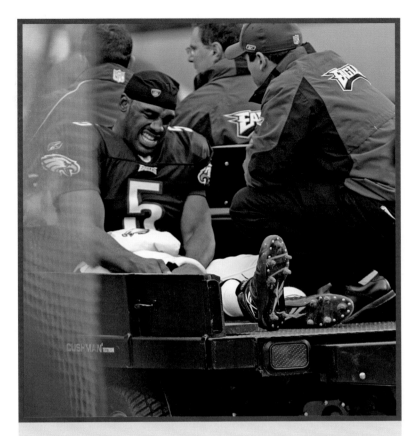

Donovan McNabb held his right knee as he was carted off the field during a game on November 19, 2006, against the Tennessee Titans. For the third time in his career, McNabb missed a significant part of a season because of injury.

son's future with the team. After all, this was the third time that Donovan's season had been cut short by an injury and a backup quarterback had to replace him. "If they win the Super Bowl without my son," Wilma wrote, according to *Philadelphia Inquirer* reporter Bob Brookover, "what would be the real outcome with the fans? Will they crucify him? Maybe then the trade talks would begin." Brookover speculated in his newspaper article that McNabb might want to be traded because the Eagles seemed so happy with Garcia. But McNabb told him, "I do not want to be traded. I plan on getting myself back healthy … and ready to go. I am a Philadelphia Eagle, and I will continue to be a Philadelphia Eagle, hopefully, for years and years to come. Hopefully I'll retire as an Eagle."

Over the winter, McNabb's recovery from his knee injury seemed to be progressing smoothly. "The leg is getting stronger," he told Marc Narducci of *The Philadelphia Inquirer.* "I was running in the [swimming] pool and am doing some running on land now." McNabb had been working out at his home in Arizona. "I have somewhat of a limp and am trying to eliminate that, and I think that just comes from not having run [on land] for a while." The Eagles, however, were taking no chances. In the 2007 draft, Philadelphia selected quarterback Kevin Kolb from the University of Houston in the second round. The Eagles gave him a four-year contract worth more than $2.5 million. Eight years earlier, the Eagles had picked McNabb, who stepped into the starting quarterback position late in 1999. There was always a chance that a similar thing could happen again and Kolb might replace McNabb if he did not fully recover.

Nevertheless, McNabb's recovery continued and by May he seemed to be ahead of schedule. During a team workout in June, McNabb was fit enough to direct the offense on some plays. At the workouts, he was wearing a brace on his knee, but Reid seemed certain that McNabb would be ready to play when the 2007 season began. "My goal is to be at 100 percent by the first game," he told Tom Pedulla of *USA Today.* "Is that a stretch? I don't know, but you have to shoot high." McNabb did not expect to start in the first exhibition game. "The second game is a possibility," he added. "The third game is even more of a possibility."

Although a full recovery from the type of injury that McNabb suffered usually takes a year, he was almost back to normal in only about nine months. In the August training camp, he was directing the offense without a knee brace. Reid tried to dismiss any talk that, by drafting Kolb, the Eagles expected to trade McNabb. "People read into that that I'm

With a brace on his knee, Donovan McNabb threw during afternoon practice at training camp in August 2007. Full recovery from the injury that McNabb suffered typically took a year, but he was back playing after only nine months.

trying to replace a quarterback," Reid told Ben Reiter of *Sports Illustrated*. "But my hope is that Donovan has 10 more great years." And tight end L.J. Smith added that he was very happy to see McNabb out on the field again.

As McNabb predicted, he did not play in the Eagles' first preseason game, which they lost to the Baltimore Ravens 29-3. In the second exhibition game, however, McNabb played for 13 minutes against the Carolina Panthers, completing six passes for 138 yards in a 27-10 victory. His performance included an impressive play-action fake and a pass to receiver Kevin Curtis that gained 27 yards. As another receiver, Jason Avant, told *Philadelphia Daily News* reporter Les Bowen, "We've been practicing with him and we knew that he still can play, still can do everything, still move well. We wanted to come out and play with some emotion. ... We did that, and he looked great." McNabb believed that he had played well. "It wasn't a test for me at all. I knew I could play. ... I think we have a long way to go, but it's still exciting to see what we're able to do."

In the third exhibition game, McNabb played through much of the first half in a loss to the Pittsburgh Steelers, throwing for only 60 yards and suffering two sacks. As the regular season was about to begin, McNabb told *USA Today* reporter Tom Pedulla that he hoped to lead the Eagles to the Super Bowl. "That's been my mind-set from my second year," McNabb explained, "because nobody remembers who finishes second and nobody cares."

DOES McNABB HAVE WHAT IT TAKES?

But McNabb's plan to reach the Super Bowl got off to a rocky start as Philadelphia lost the first game of the 2007 season to Green Bay. It was a close game, 16-13, and McNabb threw for 184 yards and a touchdown, completing almost half of his passes. He seemed to move easily across the field, and his knee appeared to be entirely healed. But he had hoped to start the season with a victory.

The Eagles' fans felt the same way, and they were highly critical of McNabb's performance. "Come on McNabb, it's time to finish the job," they yelled from the stands. They expected him to lead the team to a Super Bowl. But Philadelphia also dropped its second game—to the Washington Redskins—and the pressure on McNabb intensified. A few days after the game, an interview that McNabb taped during training camp appeared on the HBO program *Real Sports*. In the interview, McNabb said that black quarterbacks were being held to a higher standard than white quarterbacks. "It's just reality," he said. "It's something that I've been part of and other quarterbacks before me and after me have been part of."

In the third game of the season, however, McNabb showed that he was up to the test, completing 18 passes in a row, in a victory over the Detroit Lions. The Eagles rolled up 42 points in the first half on the way to a 56-21 triumph. McNabb finished 21 of 26 for 381 yards, with four touchdown passes. Three of those went to wide receiver Kevin Curtis, who scored on passes of 68, 43, and 12 yards. McNabb also completed a **screen pass** to running back Brian Westbrook, who took it in for a 43-yard touchdown.

McNabb, however, was still considered highly controversial in Philadelphia, largely based on his comments about black quarterbacks. He did not apologize. "What's been said has been said," he told Jarrett Bell of *USA Today*. Bell described him as a "lightning rod" constantly attracting controversy, based on his run-in with Terrell Owens, his conflict with Rush Limbaugh, and even his mother Wilma's questioning whether Philadelphia fans might prefer Jeff Garcia over her son. The controversy, though, did not seem to bother McNabb, who concentrated on his performance on the football field.

But in the next game, against the Giants, Philadelphia failed to score a single touchdown and McNabb was sacked 12 times. Bouncing back in Game 5, McNabb repeatedly found Curtis as the Eagles beat the New York Jets 16-9. Still, Philadelphia had gotten off to a dismal 2–3 start.

Under pressure from two Lions defenders, Donovan McNabb let a pass fly during the Eagles' third game of the 2007 season. The Eagles trounced the Lions 56-21 for their first win, as McNabb threw for 381 yards and four touchdowns.

The season did not get much better, as the Eagles suffered an embarrassing loss to the Dallas Cowboys, 38-17, in early November. McNabb managed only one touchdown pass and suffered two interceptions. "I don't think anyone did a good job, starting with me," Coach Reid told reporter Joe Drape of *The New York Times.* "We have to just keep it together. I know we're better than that. Everyone has to pull together and then we'll be fine."

In their next game, the Eagles managed to defeat the Washington Redskins, after coming from behind and scoring

COACH ANDY REID

Even with a disappointing season in 2007, Andy Reid has been the most successful coach in the history of the Philadelphia Eagles. He had won more games and had more playoff victories than any Eagles coach before him. Born in Los Angeles, California, in 1958, Reid graduated from John Marshall High School and Brigham Young University, where he was an offensive lineman on the football team. During the 1980s, Reid was an offensive line coach with several college teams before joining the Green Bay Packers in 1992. Five years later, he became the Packers' quarterback coach, working closely with Brett Favre. As a result of his success in Green Bay, he was hired by the Eagles in 1999—the same year that McNabb joined the team.

The following is Reid's record with the Eagles:

YEAR	WON	LOST	PLAYOFF RESULTS
1999	5	11	
2000	11	5	Won wild card playoffs
			Lost divisional playoffs
2001	11	5	Won wild card playoffs
			Won divisional playoffs
			Lost conference championship
2002	12	4	Won divisional playoffs
			Lost conference championship
2003	12	4	Won divisional playoffs
			Lost conference championship
2004	13	3	Won divisional playoffs
			Won conference championship
			Lost Super Bowl XXXIX
2005	6	10	
2006	10	6	Won wild card playoffs
			Lost divisional playoffs
2007	8	8	

two touchdowns near the end of the game. McNabb completed a pass to Westbrook who ran 57 yards for the winning score—capping a 20-point fourth quarter in the 33-25 win. "We need to feed off this," McNabb told Skip Wood of *USA Today*. "This says a lot about our team, says a lot about our coaching staff."

But in the next game, against the Miami Dolphins in mid-November, McNabb suffered a sprained ankle following a blitz by the Dolphins' defense. McNabb was forced to leave in the second quarter, and he was replaced by backup quarterback A.J. Feeley. (Garcia had signed with Tampa Bay in the off-season.) Although McNabb was back by December, the Eagles lost to the New York Giants. Nevertheless, he led Philadelphia to victories against Dallas, New Orleans, and Buffalo at the end of the season, and the Eagles finished at 8–8. Philadelphia, however, failed to make the playoffs.

After a string of successful years in Philadelphia, McNabb's future seemed open to question. Eagles fans had never been completely satisfied with their team's draft pick in 1999. Although the fans seemed to change their minds as McNabb led the team repeatedly to the playoffs and to a Super Bowl appearance, doubts continued to surface when he was injured and the Eagles failed to have a winning season in 2005 and 2007. After the 2007 season, there was much speculation that McNabb would be traded. Still, in the spring of 2008, both McNabb and Andy Reid said that McNabb would continue to play for the Eagles. In a radio interview in April 2008, McNabb said he wanted to play in Philadelphia for "at least another six or seven years."

"Not too many quarterbacks have been here past probably 12 years," McNabb added. "I definitely look to surpass that and bring a Super Bowl here to Philadelphia like I told them I would."

DONOVAN McNABB
Position: Quarterback

FULL NAME:
Donovan Jamal McNabb
BORN: **November 25, 1976,**
Chicago, Illinois
HEIGHT: **6'2"**

WEIGHT: **240 lbs.**
COLLEGE: **Syracuse**
TEAMS: **Philadelphia**
Eagles (1999–present)

YEAR	TEAM	G	COMP	ATT	PCT	YD	Y/A	TD	INT
1999	PHI	12	106	216	49.1	948	4.4	8	7
2000	PHI	16	330	569	58.0	3,365	5.9	21	13
2001	PHI	16	285	493	57.8	3,233	6.6	25	12
2002	PHI	10	211	361	58.4	2,289	6.3	17	6
2003	PHI	16	275	478	57.5	3,216	6.7	16	11
2004	PHI	15	300	469	64.0	3,875	8.3	31	8
2005	PHI	9	211	357	59.1	2,507	7.0	16	9
2006	PHI	10	180	316	57.0	2,647	8.4	18	6
2007	PHI	14	291	473	61.5	3,324	7.0	19	7
TOTAL		118	2,189	3,732	58.7	25,404	6.8	171	79

(continues)

(continued)

RUSHING

YEAR	ATT	YD	Y/A	TDS
1999	47	313	6.7	0
2000	86	629	7.3	6
2001	82	482	5.9	2
2002	63	460	7.3	6
2003	71	355	5.0	3
2004	41	220	5.4	3
2005	25	55	2.2	1
2006	32	212	6.6	3
2007	50	236	4.7	0
TOTAL	**497**	**2,962**	**6.0**	**24**

CHRONOLOGY

1976 November 25: Born in Chicago, Illinois.

1984 McNabb family moves to Dolton, Illinois.

1990 Donovan enters Mt. Carmel High School in Chicago.

1992 Named starting quarterback at Mt. Carmel.

1994 Receives football scholarship to Syracuse University.

1995 Leads Syracuse to a 10–2 record and a victory in the Gator Bowl; voted Big East Rookie of the Year.

1996 Voted Big East Offensive Player of the Year; Syracuse defeats University of Houston in the Liberty Bowl.

1997 Is again named the Big East Offensive Player of the Year; Syracuse wins Big East title.

1998 For third straight year, is named Big East Offensive Player of the Year; for second season in a row, Syracuse takes Big East title.

1999 Drafted by the Philadelphia Eagles with the second pick in the first round; gets first start in Week 10 against the Washington Redskins and leads Eagles to a 35-28 come-from-behind victory.

2000 McNabb leads Eagles to 11-5 season, a complete turnaround from the previous season's 5-11 mark.

2001 McNabb leads Eagles to NFC East division title.

2002 January 27: Eagles lose to the Rams, 29-24, in the NFC Championship Game.
Signs new contract worth $115 million over 12 years.
November 17: Breaks ankle in a game against the Arizona Cardinals.
Eagles finish the season at 12–4 and win NFC East.

2003 January 19: Eagles lose to the Buccaneers, 27-10, in the NFC Championship Game.

Marries Raquel-Ann Sarah Nurse.

Guides Eagles to a 12–4 season and the NFC East title.

2004　January 18 Eagles lose to the Panthers, 14-3, in the NFC Championship Game.

Eagles acquire wide receiver Terrell Owens to add strength to the offense.

McNabb leads Eagles to a 13–3 season and the NFC East title; is named NFC Offensive Player of the Year.

2005　January 23 Eagles win the NFC Championship, beating Atlanta 27-10.

TIMELINE

1976
Born November 25 in Chicago, Illinois

1995
Voted Big East Conference Rookie of the Year

1998
Named Big East Offensive Player of the Year for third straight year

1976

1999

1994
Receives football scholarship to Syracuse University

1999
Drafted by the Philadelphia Eagles as the overall No. 2 pick

February 6 McNabb and the Eagles lose the Super Bowl 24-21 to the New England Patriots.

After several conflicts, Eagles suspend Owens.

McNabb suffers a sports hernia and misses last seven games of the season; the Eagles fall to 6–10.

2006 McNabb injures a ligament in his knee and misses part of season; Eagles win NFC East.

2007 **January 13** Eagles lose in the playoffs to the New Orleans Saints.

McNabb and Eagles finish at 8–8.

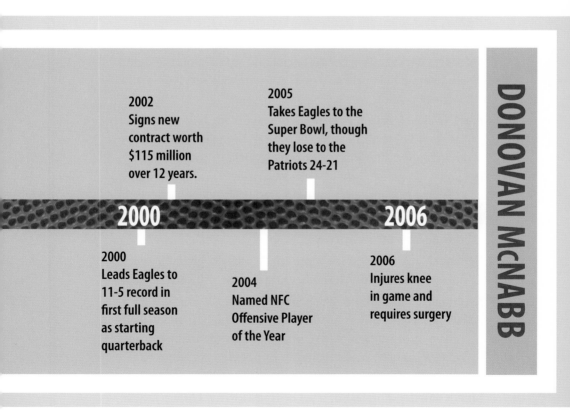

2002
Signs new contract worth $115 million over 12 years.

2005
Takes Eagles to the Super Bowl, though they lose to the Patriots 24-21

2000

2006

2000
Leads Eagles to 11-5 record in first full season as starting quarterback

2004
Named NFC Offensive Player of the Year

2006
Injures knee in game and requires surgery

DONOVAN McNABB

GLOSSARY

Achilles tendon   The tendon that joins the muscles in the calf of the leg to the bone of the heel.

American Football Conference (AFC)   One of two conferences in the National Football League. The AFC was established after the NFL merged with the American Football League (AFL) in 1970.

blitz   In this defensive play, the linebackers or defensive backs charge into the offensive team's backfield, hoping to sack the quarterback.

center   The offensive player who snaps the ball to start a play.

cornerback   A defensive back who lines up near the line of scrimmage across from a wide receiver. The cornerback's primary job is to disrupt passing routes, to defend against short and medium passes, and to contain the rusher on rushing plays.

defensive backs   The cornerbacks and safeties on the defensive team. Their primary goal is to prevent receivers from catching passes.

draft   The selection of collegiate players for entrance into the National Football League. Typically, the team with the worst record in the previous season picks first in the draft.

drive   A series of plays by the offensive team that frequently leads to a touchdown or a field goal.

end zone   The area between the end line and the goal line, bounded by the sidelines.

field goal   A three-point score made when a placekicker kicks the ball through the uprights of the opponent's goal.

first down   The first of a set of four downs. Usually, a team that has a first down needs to advance the ball 10 yards to receive another first down, but penalties or field position (i.e. less than 10 yards from the opposing end zone) can affect this.

fourth down   The last of a set of four downs. Unless a first down is achieved or a penalty forces a replay of the down, the team will lose control of the ball after this play. If a team does not think it can get a first down, it will often punt on fourth down or kick a field goal if close enough to do so.

fullback   An offensive player who lines up in the backfield and is generally responsible for blocking for the running back or quarterback. The fullback may also be used as a short-yardage runner.

fumble   When an offensive player loses control of the football that he is carrying.

goal line   The line at the front of the end zone. A touchdown is scored when the football breaks the plane of the goal line.

handoff   When a player gives the ball to a teammate in back or beside him, instead of passing it forward.

Heisman Trophy   An award presented annually to the most outstanding player in college football.

huddle   When teammates gather to discuss the next play.

incomplete pass   A forward pass that a player does not catch.

interception   A pass that is caught by a defensive player, giving his team the ball.

kickoff   The kick that begins a game, the second half, or overtime, or that follows a touchdown or field goal.

line of scrimmage   The imaginary line that stretches across the field and separates the two teams before the snap; before a play, teams line up on either side of the line of scrimmage.

linebacker   A player position on defense. Linebackers typically play one to six yards behind the defensive linemen. Most defenses use either three or four linebackers.

National Football Conference (NFC)   One of two conferences in the National Football League. The NFC was established after the NFL merged with the American Football League (AFL) in 1970.

no-huddle offense   A tactic in which the offense quickly lines up without huddling before the next play.

onside kick   An attempt by the kicking team to recover the ball by kicking it a short distance down the field. An onside kick must go 10 yards before a player on the kicking team can touch the ball.

option   In this type of play and offense, a mobile quarterback can choose between running the ball, handing off to another player, or passing the ball.

pass interference   An illegal play by a defender in which he tries to prevent a receiver from catching the ball.

pocket   The area of protection for the quarterback that is formed by the offensive line when he drops back to pass.

punt   A kick in which the ball is dropped and kicked before it reaches the ground. A punt usually occurs on fourth down and is designed to drive the opposing team as far back as possible before it takes possession of the ball.

quarterback   The player who directs the offense for his football team.

reception   A caught pass.

running back   An offensive player who runs with the football; also known as a tailback, halfback, or fullback.

sack   Any tackle of a quarterback by the defense behind the line of scrimmage. A sack also occurs if a defensive player forces the offense to fumble the ball out of bounds behind the scrimmage line.

safety   A defensive player who lines up in the secondary but often deeper than the cornerbacks. A safety is also a two-point score that occurs by downing an opposing ball carrier in his own end zone.

scramble   A run by the quarterback out of the pocket while his receivers try to get open. The quarterback will run till he can attempt a pass or, if that is not possible, rush for yardage himself.

screen pass   A forward pass at or behind the line of scrimmage to a receiver who is protected by a screen of blockers.

secondary   The defensive players who line up behind the linebackers and defend the pass.

sidelines   The lines marking out of bounds on each side of a football field.

signing bonus   An extra amount of money that a player receives when he signs a contract to play for a team.

snap   The handoff from the center, usually to the quarterback, to start a play.

starter   The player at a specific position who begins the game.

sudden death   An overtime game in which the team that scores first wins.

tackle   To stop the player with the ball and bring him to the ground. It also refers to a position on both the offfensive and defensive lines.

tight end   An offensive player who lines up on the line of scrimmage next to the offensive tackle. Tight ends are used as blockers during running plays and either run a route or stay in to block during passing plays.

timeout   A break in action requested by either team or one of the officials. In the NFL, each team gets three timeouts per half. The clock is stopped for a timeout.

touchdown   A play worth six points in which any part of the ball while legally in the possession of a player crosses the plane of the opponent's goal line. A touchdown allows the team a chance to score one extra point by kicking the ball through the goal posts or two points by running or passing the ball into the end zone.

two-point conversion   A scoring play immediately after a touchdown during which a team can add two points to the score instead of kicking for just one point; in a two-point conversion, the scoring team has one play to run or pass the ball into the end zone from the opponent's two-yard line.

West Coast offense   An offense that relies on short passes as the key to its success.

wide receiver   An offensive player who usually plays several yards out from the line of scrimmage and runs a passing route downfield.

wild card   A team in a conference that does not win a division title but has the next best record. In each conference, two wild-card teams make the playoffs.

yard   One yard of linear distance in the direction of one of the two goals. A field is 100 yards. Typically, a team is required to advance at least 10 yards to get a new set of downs.

BIBLIOGRAPHY

BOOKS

Bradley, Mitchell. *Donovan McNabb.* Tarrytown, N.Y.: Marshall Cavendish, 2005.

Mattern, Joanne. *Donovan McNabb: The Story of a Football Star.* Hockesson, Del.: Mitchell Lane Publishers, 2005.

Robinson, Tom. *Donovan McNabb: Leader on and off the Field.* Berkeley Heights, N.J.: Enslow Publishers, 2008.

ARTICLES

Anderson, Dave. "Sports of the Times: McNabb Is Going Home for a Feast and a Fracas." *The New York Times,* January 19, 2002.

Araton, Harvey. "Sports of the Times: The Young and Restless Seize Control." *The New York Times,* January 2, 2001.

Armstrong, Jenice. "Meet the Future Mrs. Donovan McNabb." *Philadelphia Daily News,* May 29, 2002.

Attner, Paul. "Master of the Board." *Sporting News,* January 21, 2005.

Battista, Judy. "Heat from Eagles' Defense Too Stifling for the Vikings." *The New York Times,* September 21, 2004.

Bell, Jarrett. "Race Finish Line Draws Nearer." *USA Today,* February 2, 2005.

———. "After Rough Week, McNabb Lets It Fly." *USA Today,* September 24, 2007.

Bernstein, Viv. "Eagles Make Their Case for Tops in the NFC." *The New York Times,* December 1, 2003.

Bowen, Les. "McNabb Is Fine Against Carolina." *Philadelphia Daily News,* August 18, 2007.

Brennan, Chris and Leon Taylor. "Hot Stuff Through Boos, Cheers and Cries for MVP, Eagles QB Has Shown McNificent Class." *Philadelphia Daily News,* November 28, 2000.

Bradley, Michael. "A Sports Hernia Is a Major Pain, and It Only Gets Worse." *Sporting News,* October 21, 2005.

Brewer, Jerry. "Prosperity Was Tough on Eagles." *The Philadelphia Inquirer,* September 12, 2000.

Brookover, Bob. "Disarmed." *The Philadelphia Inquirer,* February 2, 2005.

———. "Meet the Press." *The Philadelphia Inquirer,* February 1, 2007.

Brown, Clifton., "McNabb Endures Irregular Season and Sets Sights on Elusive Ring." *The New York Times,* January 11, 2004.

———. "Owens' Sideshow Disrupts Eagles' Camp." *The New York Times,* August 2, 2005.

———. "Like a Good Neighbor, Owens Mends Fences." *The New York Times,* November 9, 2005.

———. "The Eagles' Team Unity Has Been Transformed into Brotherly Strife." *The New York Times,* November 13, 2005.

———. "Early End to Season for McNabb." *The New York Times,* November 22, 2005.

"Browns Push, but Can't Topple, the Undefeated Eagles." *The New York Times,* October 28, 2004.

Bruton, Mike. "Charismatic McNabb Is Making a Big Pitch off the Field." *The Philadelphia Inquirer,* June 28, 2001.

Bykofsky, Stu. "McNabbed." *Philadelphia Daily News,* May 18, 2002.

Caldwell, Dave. "Eagles Win Sixth Straight, but Show Assortment of Holes." *The New York Times,* November 24, 2003.

———. "McNabb Has Been Here, But Hasn't Done That." *The New York Times,* January 17, 2004.

———. "McNabb Is Injured, and Then Ambushed." *The New York Times,* January 19, 2004.

Cavanaugh, Jack. "McNabb and Syracuse Give BC the Slip." *The New York Times,* October 18, 1998.

Chadiha, Jeffri, and Bill Syken. "Donovan McNabb." *Sports Illustrated,* August 8, 2005.

Corbett, Jim. "McNabb Runs, Throws Eagles to Win." *USA Today,* October 3, 2006.

Crossman, Matt. "Back on Top." *Sporting News,* December 8, 2003.

"Dungy Calls 'Monday Night' Sketch Racially Insensitive." *The New York Times,* November 18, 2004.

Drape, Joe. "Cowboys Rough Up Reid and the Eagles." *The New York Times,* November 5, 2007.

Elliot, Josh. "Celebrating the Fourth." *Sports Illustrated,* January 24, 2005.

Finley, Bill. "Eagles' Biggest Hurdle Lies Ahead." *The New York Times,* November 29, 2004.

Fitzpatrick, Frank. "McNabb Rises to the Occasion—As Usual." *The Philadelphia Inquirer,* January 20, 2002.

Freeman, Mike. "On Pro Bowl: Fasten Your Seat Belts, It's Going to Be a Bumpy Ride in the NFC." *The New York Times,* November 22, 2000.

———. "McNabb Rips Tampa Bay, and Sets His Sights on Giants." *The New York Times,* January 1, 2001.

Gargano, Anthony. "Pederson All But Concedes Starting Role Ineffective Again." *The Philadelphia Inquirer,* October 4, 1999.

———. "Chilling with McNabb." *The Philadelphia Inquirer,* December 5, 1999.

George, Thomas. "McNabb Won't Run from Demands." *The New York Times,* June 22, 2001.

———. "McNabb and Eagles Take the Initiative." *The New York Times,* September 17, 2002.

———. "Eagles' Offense Has a Free and Easy Time." *The New York Times,* September 23, 2002.

———. "NFL Quarterback Is Now a Temp Job." *The New York Times,* December 1, 2002.

Hack, Damon. "The Dynasty Is Official." *The New York Times,* February 7, 2005.

———. "Eagles (and Fans) Seek Answers After McNabb Misfires Again." *The New York Times,* September 15, 2003.

———. "McNabb and the Eagles Are Where the Lions Want to Be." *The New York Times,* September 27, 2004.

Hayes, Marcus. "McNabb Clearly More at Ease." *Philadelphia Daily News,* April 29, 2000.

———. "McNabb's Commitment Is Beginning to Pay Off." *Philadelphia Daily News,* May 1, 2000.

———. "Packers Bad, Eagles Worse." *Philadelphia Daily News,* September 18, 2000.

Horn, John and Jennifer York. "Black Biography: Donovan McNabb." *Biography and Much More from Answers.com.* Available online at *http://www.answers.com/topic/donovan-mcnabb.*

Iacobelli, Pete. "Freshman QB Sparks Syracuse to Rout of Clemson in Gator Bowl." *Associated Press, The Philadelphia Inquirer,* January 2, 1996.

King, Peter. "Super Effort." *Sports Illustrated,* January 31, 2005.

Klein, Michael. "Eagles' McNabb Weds College Girlfriend." *The Philadelphia Inquirer,* June 22, 2002.

Litsky, Frank. "Syracuse Encounters Other Side of Upset." *The New York Times,* September 10, 1995.

Longman, Jeré, "McNabb Is the Maestro of Creative Chaos." *The New York Times,* January 4, 2002.

———. "The Pack Can't Keep Up with the Soaring Eagles." *The New York Times,* December 6, 2004.

———. "Philadelphia Is Nervous as Eagles Move On." *The New York Times,* January 17, 2005.

Marcus, Henry. "Donovan McNabb Taking the Hits After Eagles' Super Bowl Loss." *New York Amsterdam News,* February 10, 2005.

"McNabb Can't Outrun Bitter Taste of Title Game Loss." *USA Today,* January 30, 2003.

Narducci, Marc. "McNabb: 'I've Got His Back.'" *The Philadelphia Inquirer,* February 18, 2007.

"NFL Roundup: McNabb Disputes Illness Claim." *The New York Times,* February 10, 2005.

"NFL Week 4." *The New York Times,* September 25, 2000.

"NFL Week 10." *The New York Times,* November 6, 2000.

"NFL Week 15." *The New York Times,* December 11, 2000.

Nobles, Charlie. "Syracuse Defeats Miami to Take Big East Title." *The New York Times,* November 30, 1997.

———. "Syracuse's Popular Quarterback Says Goodbye." *The New York Times,* December 29, 1998.

———."Philadelphia Wins Ninth in a Row." *The New York Times,* December 16, 2003.

"Not Just Donovan McNabb's Mom." *The Early Show*, Available online at *http://www.cbsnews.com/stories/2005/01/27/earlyshow/leisure/celebspot/main669721.shtml*

"Owens Trashes McNabb in New Book." *NBC10.com*, Available online at *http://www.nbc10.com/print/9474176/detail.html.*

Parrillo, Ray. "An Opening Orange Crush/Syracuse Pops Wisconsin in The Kickoff Classic." *The Philadelphia Inquirer,* August 25, 1997.

"Patriots Hold Off Eagles to Win Super Bowl XXXIX." *ESPN.com*, February 6, 2005. Available online at *http://sports.espn.go.com/nfl/recap?gameId=250206021.*

Pedulla, Tom. "Eagles QB Has Big Stats Despite Stabbing Feeling." *USA Today,* October 7, 2005.

———. "Smiling in Broad Daylight." *USA Today,* September 8, 2006.

———. "In Throwback, Garcia, 36, Provides Eagles an Airlift." *USA Today,* December 22, 2006.

———. "McNabb Is Looking Ahead—and over His Shoulder." *USA Today,* July 30, 2007.

———. "McNabb Still Man in Charge." *USA Today,* September 7, 2007.

Picker, David. "McNabb Tosses Aside Sluggish Start and Lifts Philadelphia." *The New York Times,* November 22, 2004.

"Plus: College Football—Senior Bowl; McNabb Impresses Coaches and Scouts." *The New York Times,* January 23, 1999.

Popper, Steve. "Giants and the Winds Bring Down McNabb." *The New York Times,* October 30, 2000.

———. "McNabb Aces Tests in Delivering Title." *The New York Times,* December 31, 2001.

Reiter, Ben. "Ready to Make a Move." *Sports Illustrated,* August 22, 2007.

Rhoden, William. "A Study in Orange and Family: McNabb's Excellent Adventure." *The New York Times,* August 25, 1996.

———. "McNabb and Syracuse Aim for a New Level of Success." *The New York Times,* August 5, 1998.

Roberts, Selena. "Throw in the Towel? Not in the NFL." *The New York Times,* November 20, 2002.

Sheridan, Phil. "McNabb Set to Prove Himself Again." *The Philadelphia Inquirer,* April 18, 1999.

———. "McNabb Makes Right Moves." *The Philadelphia Inquirer,* April 24, 1999.

———. "Holdout Headache/McNabb Disavows Race Issue." *The Philadelphia Inquirer,* July 28, 1999.

———. "Rookie McNabb Sparks Eagles to Win." *The Philadelphia Inquirer,* September 3, 1999.

———. "McNabb Aches to Shine in QB Class of 1999." *The Philadelphia Inquirer,* October 17, 1999.

———. "Square One Eagles Regress in Blowout Loss to Carolina." *The Philadelphia Inquirer,* November 8, 1999.

———. "McNabb Practices Without Knee Brace." *The Philadelphia Inquirer,* December 28, 1999.

———. "McNabb and Receivers Are Getting into Form Early." *The Philadelphia Inquirer,* March 14, 2000.

———. "Eagles Double Their Fun." *The Philadelphia Inquirer,* November 19, 2001.

———. "Parental Advisory." *The Philadelphia Inquirer,* November 3, 2002.

Silver, Michael. "Back in Stride." *Sports Illustrated,* January 20, 2003.

Smith, Michael. "McNabb: T.O. Situation Was About Money, Power." *ESPN.com.* Available online at *http://sports.espn. go.com/espn/print?id=2315565&type=story.*

Stellino, Vito. "Patriots Snap Fourth-Quarter Tie to Win Their Third Title in Four Years." *The Times-Union.* Available online at *http://www.jacksonville.com/tu-online/stories/020705/sup_17903934.shtml.*

Thamel, Pete. "Work Ethic Honed in Two Sports at Syracuse." *The New York Times,* January 11, 2004.

Wallace, William. "McNabb Unfurls a Knack to Lead." *The New York Times,* October 31, 1995.

———. "McNabb Making His Coach Nervous." *The New York Times,* October 1, 1996.

Wilbon, Michael. "Soup to Nuts, McNabb's Mom Has the Whole Package." *The Washington Post,* February 7, 2005.

Wood, Skip. "McNabb Feels at Ease with His Receivers." *USA Today,* October 9, 2006.

———."Eagles' Play Does Talking." *USA Today,* November 12, 2007.

WEB SITES

"Donovan McNabb Biography," *JockBio.com*
http://www.jockbio.com/Bios/McNabb/McNabb_bio.html.

The Donovan McNabb Foundation
http://www.mcnabbfoundation.org/.

"Donovan McNabb Player Page," *Sports Illustrated*
http://sportsillustrated.cnn.com/football/nfl/players/4650.

"Fatherhood in the NFL: Mr. Samuel McNabb," *In Search of Fatherhood*
http://globalfatherhooddialogue.blogspot.com/2007/04/fatherhood-in-nfl-mr-samuel-mcnabb.html.

FURTHER READING

BOOKS

Bass, Tom. *Youth Football Skills & Drills.* New York: McGraw-Hill, 2005.

Didinger, Ray, and Robert Lyons. *The Eagles Encyclopedia.* Philadelphia: Temple University Press, 2005.

Gordon, Robert. *Game of My Life—Philadelphia Eagles: Memorable Stories of Eagles Football.* Champaign, Ill.: Sports Publishing, LLC, 2007.

Long, Howie and John Czarnecki. *Football for Dummies.* New York: John Wiley and Sons, 2007.

McDonough, Will. *The NFL Century: The Complete Story of the National Football League, 1920–2000.* New York: Smithmark, 1999.

Palmer, Pete, et al. *The ESPN Pro Football Encyclopedia.* New York: Sterling Publishing, 2007.

WEB SITES

National Football Players Fathers Association

http://www.nfpfa.org

The Official Site of the National Football League

http://www.nfl.com

The Official Site of the Philadelphia Eagles

http://www.philadelphiaeagles.com

The Official Website of Donovan McNabb

http://donovanmcnabb.com

Pro Football Reference

http://www.pro-football-reference.com

Professional Football Players Mothers Association

http://www.pfpma.org

PICTURE CREDITS

INDEX

ABOUT THE AUTHOR

RICHARD WORTH holds a B.A. and an M.A. from Trinity College, where he studied colonial American history, and he is currently a volunteer teacher of writing to third and fourth graders. His book, *Gangs and Crime*, was included on the New York Public Library's 2003 Best Book for the Teen Age list. Worth is the author of several books for middle-grade readers and young adults, including *Henry VIII*, *Westward Expansion and Manifest Destiny*, *The Spanish Inquisition*, *American Slave Trade*, and *Plantation Life*.